The Ignatian Way

KEY ASPECTS OF JESUIT SPIRITUALITY

Charles J. Healey, SJ

Paulist Press
New York/Mahwah, NJ

IMPRIMI POTEST: Reverend Thomas J. Regan, S.J., Provincial of the New England Province of Jesuits, January 12, 2008.

Cover and book design by Lynn Else

Cover art: Saint Ignatius Founder of the Jesuits. Stained glass window. Used with permission.

Library of Congress Cataloging-in Publication Data

Healey, Charles J.
    The Ignatian way : key aspects of Jesuit spirituality / Charles J. Healey.
        p. cm.
    Includes bibliographical references (p.   ).
    ISBN 978-0-8091-4616-1 (alk. paper)
    1. Ignatius, of Loyola, Saint, 1491–1556. Exercitia spiritualia. 2. Spirituality—Catholic Church. 3. Catholic Church—Doctrines. 4. Spiritual exercises. I. Title.
    BX2179.L8H43 2009
    248.3—dc22
                                                                                2009011670

Published by Paulist Press
997 Macarthur Boulevard
Mahwah, New Jersey 07430

www.paulistpress.com

Printed and bound in the
United States of America

CONTENTS

CONTENTS

CONTENTS

PREFACE

The spirituality that flows from the life and writings of Saint Ignatius Loyola (c. 1491–1556) has had a widespread influence since the time of his death. This is especially true at the present time, given the renewed interest in Christian spirituality in general and the particular interest that has emerged in such areas as spiritual direction, the directed retreat movement, personal and group discernment, and the making of various forms of the retreat in everyday life.

This renewed interest has also given birth to a number of important studies dealing with various aspects of Ignatian spirituality. Most of them, however, have been of a specialized and scholarly nature, focusing for the most part on certain areas and topics of Ignatian spirituality. Although these studies have been of great significance, they are often too detailed for those whose knowledge of Ignatian studies is limited and for those who are looking for a more general introduction to the many aspects of Ignatian spirituality.

This book provides an introduction to Ignatian spirituality. It seeks to respond to the needs of those who are looking for a book that will provide a readable and not overly detailed overview of the many aspects of the spirituality associated with Saint Ignatius of Loyola. They might include such groups as those men and women who are collaborating with the Jesuits in educational institutions or various other apostolic works and wish to know more about the spirituality that forms the guiding spirit for these apostolates;

alumni of Jesuit schools; those who have been exposed to this spirituality through retreats and spiritual direction and wish to pursue it further for their own spiritual development; those pondering a possible vocation to the Society of Jesus; or those who are simply seeking more exposure to this spirituality for various other reasons.

Any particular form of Christian spirituality has to be rooted, of course, in the Gospels and the saving mystery of Christ's death and resurrection. There can be some differences, however, arising from particular emphases, the unique charism and experiences of the founders of schools of spirituality, and the needs of the church and society at a certain period of history. Thus, we can speak of Benedictine, Franciscan, Dominican, Carmelite, and Salesian spiritualities, to mention a few. Ignatian spirituality is marked by a strong apostolic thrust and orientation. It is particularly suited, therefore, for those who are actively engaged in various forms of ministry and service and are seeking to find God in their lives and work. These people would include members of the Society of Jesus itself, diocesan priests and seminarians, religious men and women in active congregations, and the many dedicated and spiritually motivated laymen and laywomen.

When we speak of Ignatian spirituality, we realize that it is intimately linked to the spirit and vision of the founder of the Society of Jesus, Saint Ignatius of Loyola. But it is important to keep in mind that Ignatian spirituality is broader than the term *Jesuit spirituality*. Ignatian spirituality certainly animates the lives and apostolic endeavors of Jesuits, the members of the religious order that Saint Ignatius founded; but it is not limited to them alone. His spirituality is a gift to the whole church and has easily and readily been adopted and appropriated by many others, particularly by those whose lives have a strong apostolic thrust. Although the focus in the following chapters is more on Jesuit spirituality, it is hoped that the larger meaning of Ignatian spirituality will be constantly kept in mind.

PREFACE

The following chapters seek to develop the key aspects of Ignatian spirituality. The first chapter focuses on Saint Ignatius's early spiritual journey and his personal experiences of God's grace in his life, since so much of Ignatian spirituality flows from this source. The second chapter concentrates on his later years and his legacy as a religious leader, writer, and mystic. Chapter 3 treats the *Spiritual Exercises* of Saint Ignatius, his well-known and significant gift and legacy to the entire church and a work that is so central to Ignatian spirituality. The following two chapters explore in more depth two key aspects of the *Spiritual Exercises*, namely, Ignatian prayer and Ignatian discernment. Chapter 6 treats the second great source of the spiritual teaching of Saint Ignatius, the *Constitutions of the Society of Jesus*. Since any spirituality must be able and ready to adapt itself to the changing conditions of the times while remaining faithful to its heritage, the seventh chapter focuses on the issues and challenges that affect Ignatian spirituality in contemporary times. Finally, chapter 8 is devoted to the concrete, lived-out expression of Ignatian spirituality with brief profiles of some representative Jesuits.

In conclusion, I wish to express my sincere appreciation to those who read over the text of the manuscript and made helpful suggestions: Sr. Mary T. Sweeney, SCH; Robert G. Doherty, SJ; George L. Drury, SJ; James A. Egan, SJ; Paul F. Harman, SJ; and Richard J. Hauser, SJ.

1

IGNATIUS'S JOURNEY

Any account of Ignatian spirituality has to begin with the life of Saint Ignatius of Loyola.[1] So much of Ignatian spirituality flows from this source, particularly from his own personal experiences of God's grace that worked so powerfully in his life. Ignatius's own *Autobiography* is a rich source for this.[2] After many requests from fellow Jesuits, Ignatius finally agreed late in his life to dictate an account of his spiritual experiences to one of the early Jesuits, Luis da Camara, focusing primarily on the period extending from his conversion in 1521 to the beginnings of the Society of Jesus in Rome in 1538. Although it does not include anything about the final years of Ignatius, it is a valuable account of his own experiences of God during a crucial period of his life. Written in a simple, straightforward way, it has a unique power to convey the key points of the saint's spiritual journey during what is usually referred to as the pilgrim years.

This chapter focuses on these early adult years of Ignatius of Loyola, the years from his conversion experience as a soldier in 1521 until his election as the first superior general of the newly established Society of Jesus in 1541.[3] The following chapter treats the last fifteen years of his life that he spent in Rome.

Ignatius of Loyola (c. 1491–1556) lived in a period of transition—a time of great expansion in the world and great change in the church. The year after the birth of Ignatius Columbus would be journeying to the Americas and opening up the New World, and while Ignatius was still a young man, Martin Luther would be nailing his theses on indulgences to the door of the church at Wittenberg and ushering in the Protestant Reformation with its far-reaching results for both church and state. This is the somewhat turbulent historical context in which the spiritual odyssey of Ignatius took shape, an odyssey that would have profound repercussions for him and others.

1. The Soldier

The information about Ignatius's early years is scanty. Born around 1491 at the castle of Loyola in the Basque province of Guipúzcoa in Spain, Inigo (as he was called in his early years) was attracted at an early age to a military life. At the household of the chief treasurer of Queen Isabella, the young Ignatius received the basic formation of a Spanish gentleman and courtier. It was a life marked, as he tells us in his *Autobiography*, "with a great and vain desire to win honor," and he delighted in the military exercises. In 1517, after the death of his patron at the royal court, Ignatius went to Navarre in northern Spain and became part of the command of the duke of Najera, the viceroy of Navarre who was in charge of its defense.

In 1521 the French, seeking to regain the area King Ferdinand had conquered and annexed in 1512, marched on this frontier area and occupied the city of Pamplona. Ignatius rallied the troops and bravely defended the citadel at Pamplona until he was seriously wounded; one leg was broken and the other was shattered by a cannonball. The French treated the gallant soldier with respect and courtesy and had him transported by stretcher to his ancestral castle at Loyola. Doctors there sought to remedy the mistakes the French doctors had made in setting the broken bones and they operated again on the leg. He rallied from this operation, which almost took his life, but again it proved unsuccessful and he was left with a deformity in the leg. This was something he could not endure, for it would mean the end of his dreams of winning honor and glory as a soldier and a knight, and so he insisted upon another operation, even though it entailed even more agony this time. The operation was almost a complete success but it called for an extended period of convalescence.

This period of convalescence was to be the turning point of his life, for he would rise from his sick bed a profoundly changed person, seeking a totally new direction in his life. During his days of enforced idleness, he sought books to read. He would have preferred the romances he was accustomed to reading, but the only books available were the *Life of Christ* by the Carthusian, Ludolph of Saxony, and the popular medieval lives of the saints known as *The Golden Legend* by a thirteenth-century Dominican, Jacopo de Voragine. Under God's grace, these books were to affect him deeply and to stir up many holy thoughts and desires. Using his imagination, Ignatius would see Christ as a King who calls his followers to engage in a warfare and the saints as knights in his special service, and he dreamed of emulating the deeds of the great mendicant saints of the thirteenth century, Francis of Assisi and Dominic. But these reflections alternated in his mind with his dreams of romantic and military conquests. He imagined the honors he would win at the royal court and what he would do in the service of a certain lady, the words he would say to her, and the armed exploits he would perform in her service. These latter thoughts gave him pleasure while he dwelt upon them but they later left him feeling dry and dissatisfied. He slowly recognized, on the other hand, that the holy thoughts and desires brought him a peace and consolation that remained with him long after his reading and reflection. Gradually he came to an awareness of the sources of these interior movements and he began to discern and distinguish those that were from a divine source and those that were not. He came to look upon the human person as a battleground between the forces of good and the forces of evil, and he clearly saw that a choice and a commitment had to be made. Moved by God's grace, Ignatius committed himself generously to God's service with that energy and devotion with which he had previously pursued his courtly and military career.

2. The Pilgrim

The months of convalescence had produced a profound conversion of heart in Ignatius. Thus, when he was able to set out from the castle of Loyola, it was with the firm resolve to journey to the Holy Land as a pilgrim. His first stop was at the famous Benedictine monastery of Montserrat in Spain. After some days of prayer, he made a general confession of his life and then symbolically left his sword and dagger with his confessor to be placed in the church on the altar of Our Lady. He spent the night in prayer before the altar, an act that was reminiscent of the knightly vigil of prayer before battle. No longer would it be military battle for Ignatius, but spiritual warfare in which he would engage himself totally and heroically.

Dressed as a pilgrim, Ignatius set out for the nearby town of Manresa, where he planned to spend a few days copying some notes in a spiritual journal he was keeping. As so often happens in the lives of great leaders before their periods of intense creativity and activity, he needed an extended period of withdrawal and solitude, and so the few days lengthened to almost a year. During these days, he begged for his daily bread, helped the sick in the hospital, attended daily Mass and vespers at the cathedral, spent long hours in prayer, and practiced severe penances. It was a time of many mystical graces and consolations, but it was also a time of purgation, trials, and temptations. "God was leading him like a child," he tells us in his *Autobiography*. The novice in the spiritual life was being transformed slowly and at times painfully into a master of the spiritual life. God's grace was abundant and the pilgrim cooperated generously. The *Spiritual Exercises* of Saint Ignatius stem from these days at Manresa, although they would undergo much development and revision before their final publication many years later. The core of the work goes back to the notes he kept at Manresa, the notes that flowed basically from his own prayerful experiences of God's grace working within him. This practice of making notes may have been suggested by his Benedictine confessor at Montserrat.

Toward the end of February 1523, Ignatius left Manresa and traveled by way of Barcelona and Rome to Venice, the port of embarkation for pilgrims to the Holy Land. After two months of waiting for a ship, he finally secured passage and arrived safely at Joppa. Days of great consolation and devotion followed as he visited with the other pilgrims the land hallowed by the presence of the Christ he now sought to serve so fully and generously. When the pilgrimage was over, he wanted to remain in the Holy Land and work for the conversion of the Muslims, but given the precarious situation between the Christians and the Turks, the Franciscan superior who had ecclesiastical authority kindly but firmly vetoed this plan.

3. The Student

With the collapse of his hopes to remain and labor in the Holy Land, Ignatius was forced to reassess his plans for his apostolic activity. He decided after prayer to pursue a formal education since he saw that this was so necessary for any effective apostolate. He was thirty-three years old at the time and his course of studies would involve him for the next eleven years, taking him first to Barcelona, then to the Spanish universities at Alcala and Salamanca, and finally to the University of Paris.

At Paris, a small band formed around Ignatius: Peter Faber, Francis Xavier, Simón Rodrigues, Diego Laynez, Alonso Salmeron, and Nicholás Bobadilla. At first it was a loosely formed group, bound only by ties of friendship and a common vision and set of ideals. Through his own personal influence and also by directing them in the spiritual exercises, Ignatius inspired them with his strong apostolic thrust, love of God above all things, and strong desire to serve Christ the King with a generous heart. Gradually, and after long discussion and prayer, they decided that after their studies they would remain together as a group and go and work in the Holy Land for the conversion of the Muslims. In order to strengthen their determination and their bond of unity, they decided to take three vows: poverty, chastity, and a resolve to go to the Holy Land. If this third vow proved impossible to fulfill, they would go to Rome and offer their services to the pope.

On August 15, 1534, the Feast of the Assumption of the Virgin Mary, the seven men left the Latin Quarter and walked to the small chapel dedicated to Saint Denis on the slope of Montmartre. Peter Faber, the only priest among them at the time, celebrated Mass in the crypt, and just before receiving Holy Communion each of the seven pronounced the vows. The decision to form a religious order with Ignatius at its head still lay in the future, but an important foundation stone had been laid at Montmartre and it has always been a revered moment in Jesuit history.

4. The Founder and General

The following years found Ignatius and his companions finishing their studies at the University of Paris at various times. Ignatius finished his own studies in 1535, returned to his native Spain for a short period, and then moved on to Venice. Finally, in early 1537, all seven were reunited in Venice, where they hoped to find a ship that would take them to the Holy Land. Three others had joined them in Paris and so the band now numbered ten. Ignatius was ordained to the priesthood in Venice with the others who were not already priests, and all of them spent the year in priestly work as they waited for a ship. Before traveling to the nearby towns to preach the gospel, they decided that if they were asked to identify themselves, they would say they were of the "Company of Jesus." At the end of the year, with the hostilities between Venice and the Turks making it impossible to make passage to the Holy Land, the companions decided to travel to Rome. On the journey to Rome, Ignatius stopped to pray at the little chapel at La Storta, just outside of Rome. While praying there Ignatius was graced with a vision of the Father and the Son, and he saw clearly that the Father had placed him with his Son. Ignatius was also greatly strengthened and confirmed in his plans and desires by the words of the Father, "I will be propitious to you in Rome."

The pope warmly received the pilgrim priests at Rome, and they made a deep impression in the city through their holy lives and their learning, as they continued to preach and minister to the sick. It was clear by early 1539 that they would not be able to go to the Holy Land, and so as planned earlier, they offered their services to the pope and expressed their willingness to go to the Indies or any other part of the world where there was an apostolic need.

After a month of prayer and deliberation in seeking God's will, the ten made the historic decision to form an entirely new religious order and to take a vow of obedience to one of their members. Ignatius drew up the document that summed up their purpose and aim, and the others approved it. The opening words of this document, known as the *Formula of the Institute*, form a strong link with Ignatius's particular vision and the spirit of the *Spiritual Exercises*: "Whoever desires to serve as a soldier of God beneath the banner of the cross in our Society, which we desire to be designated by the name of Jesus, and to serve the Lord alone and the Church…" The fundamental points that would be developed later in the *Constitutions of the Society of Jesus*, namely, the strong apostolic dimension, loyalty to the Holy See, a readiness to go anywhere in the world, a prompt and persevering obedience to the general that they would elect from the group, and the unique abolition of the tradition chanting in common of the Divine Office (Liturgy of the Hours) for the interest of the apostolate, were contained in this document in seed form. In general, it was a new and pioneering type of religious order and one well suited to the needs of the church at the time, with its stress on mobility and flexibility. Pope Paul III gave formal approbation on September 27, 1540, in the papal document, *Regimini militantis ecclesiae*, and during Lent of 1541, Ignatius was elected the first superior general.

For the last sixteen years of his life, Ignatius remained in Rome, fulfilling the demanding duties of general of the new order. The pilgrim years were definitely over for Ignatius, because the rapid growth and expansion of the church's new apostolic body of men required his ongoing care and supervision. These later years of Ignatius are the focus of the following chapter.

2

IGNATIUS'S LATER YEARS (1541–56)

The years in Rome as general of the new order continued to be a time of growth for Ignatius, but his attention now was directed more to the new foundation and to the challenges and opportunities that are a part of any new undertaking. He gave himself generously to the ongoing work of organization and administration that was required for the expanding numbers and the growing apostolic ministries.

In addition to this work, Ignatius also devoted himself to the task of ensuring that a written legacy was left behind. Organizational genius that he was, he clearly saw that if his vision and spirit were to remain after his death and be imparted to others, it would have to be carefully and painstakingly spelled out. What he accomplished in his own lifetime through personal contact and influence could only continue if there was a written legacy. This would be accomplished primarily through the writing of his *Spiritual Exercises* and his *Constitutions*.

Finally, during these years in Rome, Ignatius grew in holiness and was the recipient of many mystical graces in his prayer. All his external labors flowed from his abiding sense of God's presence in his life and his deep desire to serve the Divine Majesty in a spirit of generosity and magnanimity.

We can thus speak of three important dimensions in the life of Ignatius during these later years: the religious leader; the writer; and the saint and mystic.

1. The Religious Leader

During the fifteen years of Ignatius's leadership, the original ten companions would grow in number to a thousand, and the direction of the Jesuits laboring on four continents would absorb his time and energy. Shortly after the foundation of the Society of Jesus, the ten founding fathers were engaged in such varied apostolic activities as preaching and giving the spiritual exercises, acting as theologians at the Council of Trent (1545–63), serving as papal legates, teaching and lecturing, and laboring in foreign missions. Francis Xavier left Europe almost immediately after the formal formation of the group to begin his great missionary activity. The work that took him to the Indies and Japan came to an end with his death on a lonely island while he was awaiting passage to the mainland of China. Given the needs of the times, it would not be long before the work of the foreign missions as well as the running of schools would assume growing importance.

Shortly after Ignatius was chosen to lead the new apostolic order, the Society received from the pope its first church and parish, Santa Maria della Strada (Our Lady of the Road). It was an apt title for the mother church of an essentially missionary order whose main thrust was toward apostolic endeavors and worldwide missionary activity.[1] At the residence attached to the church, Ignatius, the pilgrim for so long, now found the place that would be his home until his death. This house would become under Ignatius's leadership the center of the Society of Jesus in Rome and the headquarters for all its apostolic undertakings throughout the world, for the mission of the Society was to travel to any part of the world where the vicar of Christ might send them. A recent biographer sums up this role of Ignatius very well:

> In fact, he would scarcely ever leave this place during the fifteen years of his generalship, but from the heart of his little room, he would follow the flight of his sons on the roads of the world. He would inspire them in their missionary zeal, sustain them in their battles. There, success and failure, sorrows and joys, good news and bad would blend; hundreds of companions would pass through there to be trained or to work.[2]

It is interesting to note that Ignatius placed great importance and significance on the place of letters in his role of religious leader. He quickly realized their great value in fostering a sense of unity and maintaining bonds among those who were dispersed far and wide in their apostolic labors. What could be accomplished in the monastic communities through meetings and chapters could now take place only through the letters that would link Ignatius to his fellow Jesuits. He himself was a prolific letter writer and there are in existence almost seven thousand of his letters of instruction and spiritual direction.

But in addition to his own letters, Ignatius required from his scattered companions what he referred to as *principal letters*. He wanted these letters to describe their spiritual and apostolic activities so that they could be made available to others. Since they would be shared with others and would be of a more public nature, he did ask that they be well thought out and drawn up in a careful and orderly way.[3]

In all of the vast correspondence that developed, Ignatius was greatly helped by the Spanish Jesuit, Juan de Polanco, who worked closely with him as secretary of the Society. Polanco himself soon began the practice of periodically sending out circular letters to all the members of the Society. These circular letters would make use of the principal letters that were sent to Rome from around the world and would summarize the most important of the apostolic activities of the dispersed Jesuits.

2. The Writer

The claim has never been made that Ignatius was a gifted writer or literary stylist, but the importance of the writings themselves has long been recognized. He was someone who saw the great value of communicating through the written word and the importance of leaving behind a written legacy of his spiritual vision. There was always a practical thrust and dimension to his writings that was intimately connected with his apostolic vision in the service of the Divine Majesty. The writings were for the most part connected with Ignatius's later years in Rome and it would seem best to summarize them briefly at this point chronologically.

The *Spiritual Exercises*

The *Spiritual Exercises* of Saint Ignatius is certainly the best known of all his writings. This spiritual document is foundational for Ignatius's own spiritual journey and the spirituality of all Jesuits. Much more will be said about this important work and its overall content in a later chapter, but some brief comments are in order here.

The beginnings of the *Spiritual Exercises* go back to the time Ignatius spent at Manresa in 1521, shortly after his conversion experience. He developed during these days at Manresa the habit of recording notes that described his own spiritual experiences or served as aids in his ongoing prayers and devotions. During the subsequent years he continued to make additions and revisions to the emerging text that would also aid the many people he engaged in spiritual conversation during his student years. All of his early companions at Paris made the exercises under his direction and they were the principal means he used under God's grace to lead them to a strong desire to share his apostolic vision and commitment to the service of Christ.

Thus, although the *Spiritual Exercises* were not published in a definitive form until 1548, eight years before Ignatius's death, they were being constantly revised and expanded as Ignatius's own spirituality developed and deepened. As George Ganss writes of Ignatius and his *Spiritual Exercises*:

> This small book, begun in 1522, contains the marrow of his spiritual outlook and most quickly mirrors to us the synthesis of his principles. It reveals much of his personality as well. From 1522 to about 1541 his own spirituality developed side by side with his revisions of and additions to the pages which were to become the book published in 1548, twenty-six years after its inception.[4]

It is important to keep in mind that Ignatius did *not* intend the *Spiritual Exercises* to be any kind of a treatise of the spiritual life or a book to be picked up and read as an ordinary book. Intended primarily for the one directing the exercises, it is simply a series of spiritual exercises (prayers, meditations, contemplations, instructions) that are to be carried out by a retreatant who seeks to find God's will in prayer under the guidance of a director.

The *Constitutions*

The writing of the *Constitutions of the Society of Jesus* occupied a central place during the years Ignatius served as leader of the new religious order. Ignatius attached the highest priority to their composition, for they were to spell out in an organized and coherent form the basic thrust of his vision and inspiration for the order he had founded.

The final published version came only after a number of years and it developed through various stages. The beginnings go back to the decision made by the ten founding fathers in 1539 that they would form a new religious order. With the assistance of the others, Ignatius drew up a brief document that was to be submitted for papal approval. It has become known as the *Formula of the Institute* and consists of five chapters, each not more than a paragraph long. This document was incorporated in the papal bull, *Regimini militantis ecclesiae*, in which Pope Paul III formally approved the Society on September 27, 1540. The *Formula of the Institute* became the fundamental Rule for the new order and it authorized the superior general to develop and expand this foundational document.

Ignatius assumed this responsibility when he himself was elected superior general in 1541 and considered it one of his main responsibilities throughout the fifteen years of his leadership. The writing was greatly facilitated when Juan Polanco became secretary of the Society in 1547, since he brought his considerable literary and organizational skills to the work of composition. Another early Jesuit who played an extremely important role in this painstaking work was Jerónimo Nadal. When a preliminary text was completed in 1552, Nadal traveled extensively to the Jesuit communities in Sicily, Spain, Portugal, Germany, and Austria, explaining and promulgating the *Constitutions* on an experimental basis. Ignatius himself continued to modify and revise the text until his death in 1556. Polanco then prepared the Latin translation from the Spanish Autograph and this was subsequently approved by the First General Congregation that was convened to elect a successor to Ignatius. Henceforth the *Constitutions* would guide the way

Jesuits lived and worked, and its significance is symbolized by the expression used by the early Jesuits: "Our Way of Proceeding."

Letters

The importance Ignatius gave to letters (not unlike the apostle Paul) as a means of fostering unity and support among the early Jesuits dispersed throughout the world has already been noted. Ignatius himself was a prolific letter writer and close to seven thousand of his letters have survived. They are a rich source of information about developments in the early Society and they also provide a great deal of information about the personality and vision of Ignatius. In his many letters of direction and guidance he seeks to apply his spiritual vision and principles to practical situations and challenges and bring people to a fuller and more generous relationship with God. As Ganss notes: "He is always trying to see things from God's point of view, and to help his correspondents to fit their lives and affairs cooperatively in God's plan of salvation for those who use their freedom wisely."[5]

Many of his thoughts and ideas found in the *Spiritual Exercises* and the *Constitutions* find their way into the pages of these letters. They are expressed in such frequently used phrases as "the service of God," "the glory of God," and "the service and praise of God." He would often close his letters with a formula such as: "I close by asking God through his infinite Goodness to give us the perfect grace to know His most holy will and to fulfill it completely." [6]

The *Autobiography*

Mention has already been made of the *Autobiography* when Ignatius's conversion and early spiritual journey were discussed. Although it focuses on Ignatius's early years, it is the last of his writ-

ings. Toward the end of his years as general superior, he acceded to
the repeated requests of his early companions that he leave some
form of a testament of his interior life and the graces he received
from God in founding the Society. He eventually dictated an
account of his life to Luis da Camara during the years 1553 and 1555.
The narration was interrupted in 1555, the year before his death, so
it is an incomplete account. It *does* cover the crucial period of his life
from the battle of Pamplona in 1521 through his first year in Rome
in 1538 and provides us with valuable information on these years.
Fortunately, the details of his interior life from 1539 to 1556 are
available from other good sources. One is the *Spiritual Diary* that he
kept for a period during his later years in Rome.

3. The Saint and Mystic

Ignatius's growth in holiness, as we have seen, was steady and
ongoing. The love of God and the strong desire to serve God generously and faithfully grew and developed constantly in his heart.
Those who came in contact with him along the paths of his spiritual journey, particularly his early Jesuit companions, attest to his
great desire to give God the central place in his life and to seek
nothing more than the fulfillment of the will of God in all the circumstances of his life. His holiness was soon recognized far and
wide. In 1622, sixty-six years after his death, Ignatius was canonized along with some other great saints of the church: his early
companion, Saint Francis Xavier; the great Carmelite mystic, Saint
Teresa of Avila; his Roman friend and founder of the Oratorians,
Saint Philip Neri; and the popular Spanish saint and patron of
farmers, Saint Isidore the Farmer (d. 1130). This distinguished
group is known in Spain as "The Five Saints."

What may not be as easily known and recognized is Ignatius's
position as one of the great Christian *mystics*. There is a close connec-

tion between the strong apostolic thrust that marked Ignatius's life and the depth of his mystical prayer. Focusing on this intimate link, Harvey Egan in his study of Ignatius's mysticism concludes: "Ignatius was an incomparable mystic whose mystical and apostolic gifts are really two sides of the same coin. Ignatius was apostolic *because* he was one of the greatest mystics the Church has even seen. His apostolic successes are the mystical expressions, the sacramental embodiment of his radical mysticism."[7]

In his *Autobiography*, Ignatius gives us some glimpses of the mystical favors he received through God's abundant graces. Among them are the many mystical illuminations he received during his days at Manresa. Shortly after his conversion, he gave priority to what is usually referred to as the vision along the banks of the river Cardonner. As Ignatius himself narrates in the third person:

> As he sat, the eyes of his understanding began to open. He beheld no vision, but he saw and understood many things, spiritual as well as those concerning faith and learning. This took place with so great an illumination that these things appeared to be something altogether new. He cannot point out the particulars of what he then understood, although they were many, except that he received a great illumination in his understanding. This was so great that in the whole course of his past life right up to his sixty-second year, if he were to gather all the helps he had received from God, and everything he knew, and add them together, he does not think that they would equal all that he received at that one time.[8]

Significant also are his remarks on the mystical graces he received much later while he was in Vicenza, Italy, preparing for ordination to the priesthood and getting ready to celebrate his first Mass. He tells us that he had many supernatural visions and much ordinary consolation, and that in all his apostolic journeys he had great supernatural visions of the kind he used to have while he was at Manresa.[9]

The last and extremely significant mystical experience that he mentions toward the end of the *Autobiography* is that which took place at La Storta. While traveling to Rome from Venice in 1539, he stopped to pray at the little church in La Storta, a few miles outside of Rome. He felt such a change in his soul while he was praying that he was convinced that God the Father had placed him with Christ and that the providential love of God would be with him in the future while he was seeking to serve Christ.[10]

No account of Ignatius's mysticism would be complete without some reference to his *Spiritual Diary*. There are extant pages from the diary Ignatius kept about his experiences of prayer during the period between February 1544 and February 1545. At that time he was directing the Society as superior general in Rome and composing the text of the *Constitutions*. He was particularly concerned about the question of canonical poverty for the Society, and he sought in prayer to find God's will in this matter and make the appropriate choice. He sought to discern God's will by carefully recording the consolations and desolations he received in his prayer. These pages clearly indicate the depth of his prayer and the mystical gifts that often accompanied it.[11]

These pages also led the Jesuit scholar, Joseph de Guibert, to write: "We are in the presence of a mystical life in the strictest sense of this term. We are in the company of a soul that is being led by God in the ways of infused contemplation to the same degree, though not in the same manner, as a Saint Francis of Assisi or a Saint John of the Cross."[12] This author goes on to describe and characterize Ignatius's mysticism as trinitarian and eucharistic in regard to its object and as a mysticism of service because of love in regard to its general orientation.

Conclusion

Before leaving this overview of the life of Ignatius, it might be helpful to summarize some of the main aspects of his spirituality that have emerged in his life. These points will be developed at greater length in the chapters that follow, especially those that treat his *Spiritual Exercises* and *Constitutions*.

We can begin with the phrase *ad majorem Dei gloriam* (for the greater glory of God), long associated with Ignatius' spirituality. The glory of God and the fulfillment of his will were uppermost in Ignatius's mind and central to his world vision. References to the glory of God and the service of the Divine Majesty appear over and over again in his letters and in the pages of the *Constitutions* and *Spiritual Exercises*. Ignatius sought to achieve the glory of God through apostolic service—through a faithful and generous service of the Divine Majesty that would take place in the church under the direction of the pope, the vicar of Christ. Service and conformity to God's will were central to Ignatius's spirituality.

The source and motivating force for this ongoing service flows from a deep and abiding love of Christ. It is a personal love of such depth and devotion that it impels a person to desire and embrace even poverty and insults so as to be more closely identified with Christ in the task of winning the world to the service and glory of God the Father. To be with Jesus in order to serve was essential for Ignatius.

It should be kept in mind that Ignatius's vision calls not only for an active person and one totally committed to one's apostolic work, but also for a person who brings a strong and abiding contemplative dimension to that work. A faith-filled dimension and perspective should permeate and be at the heart of all the activity. "Finding God in all things" and being "a contemplative in action" are the traditional expressions that signify this essential orientation.

One seeks to begin and continue this work, whatever it might be, for "the greater glory of God."

This is the particular message that emerges under God's grace from the life and vision of Saint Ignatius. It is a spiritual message in the words of de Guibert of "service through love, apostolic service for the greatest possible glory to God, a service given in generous conformity to the will of God. In the abnegation or sacrifice of all self-love and personal interest in order to follow Christ, the Leader who is ardently loved."[13] It is a spirit summed up in the prayer for generosity long associated with Saint Ignatius:

> Dearest Lord, teach me to be generous. Teach me to serve you as you deserve; to give and not to count the cost; to fight and not to heed the wound; to toil and not to seek for rest; to labor and not ask for reward save that of knowing that I am doing your will.

3

THE SPIRITUAL EXERCISES

It should be emphasized once again that Ignatius's *Spiritual Exercises* flowed from his own prayerful experience and from his growing awareness after his conversion of the many ways God's grace was working powerfully in his life.[1] The notes he kept of these graces during his days at Manresa form the basis of this spiritual classic that continued to be amplified and revised until its definitive publication in 1548. During the long years of his studies at the universities in Spain and Paris, he made use of the exercises to assist many who were seeking a deeper relationship with God in ways that were adapted to their needs. They were given in their full form to such early companions as Francis Xavier and Peter Faber and the others in the group who formed the founding fathers of the new order. Even during the busy and challenging years of his generalate, Ignatius continued to direct others in the exercises as time allowed.

The foundation in the exercises that the early Jesuit companions of Ignatius received continued as the number of Jesuits expanded. (It will be recalled that the number grew during Ignatius's years as superior general from ten to one thousand!) Jesuits made the spiritual exercises in their entirety during the initial period of training, the novitiate, and they would continue to nourish their ongoing prayer and apostolic ministries. From the very beginning, the spiritual exercises occupied a prominent role in all the apostolic ministries in which Jesuits were engaged and this has continued to the present day.[2] Thus, there is no doubt that the spiritual exercises are central to Ignatian spirituality, and for this reason we turn in this chapter to a closer look at them.

Some preliminary observations should be made here at the outset. First, the *Exercises* are basically a manual of prayer. As such they are part of the spiritual tradition that actually preceded Ignatius. Methods of prayer and various forms of spiritual exercises began to take on greater importance at the end of the Middle Ages and the beginning of the Renaissance period as a means of countering a general decline of religious fervor. Thus, the chief aim of methodical forms of prayer was the renewal and reform of the Christian life, especially among the clergy and religious. The *Spiritual Exercises* of Saint Ignatius of Loyola were destined to have the greatest impact and influence, but it is important to realize that they were the culmination of earlier historical developments.[3]

An example of an earlier form of spiritual exercises and one that Ignatius most likely had some direct contact with would be that of Garcia Ximenes de Cisneros (1455–1510), the reforming abbot of the Benedictine monastery at Montserrat in Spain. He drew up a manual of spiritual exercises for his monks as a means of spiritual renewal. These helps for prayer were divided into three weeks, with each week corresponding to the traditional purgative, illuminative, and unitive ways with appropriate material for prayer drawn up for each day of the week. It will be recalled that Ignatius made a pilgrimage to Montserrat shortly after his conversion and recovery at Loyola and spent some days there in prayer under the guidance of one of the monks.

A second preliminary observation centers on the nature of the text as a literary document. It should be stressed that Ignatius did not intend the *Spiritual Exercises* to be a type of "self-help" book in which readers would hopefully find material that would assist them in their prayer and spiritual growth. These readers would be disappointed and even puzzled by its overall format. The text as we have it is intended primarily for the person who would be directing and leading others in an experience of prayer by making use of these exercises. It forms a set of instructions, guidelines, methods, and suggestions for the director who must always keep in mind that the principal director is of course the Holy Spirit. The main text of the *Exercises* is divided into what Ignatius referred to as four "weeks." For the person making the exercises in their entirety over a period of thirty days, a number of days (not necessarily corresponding to a seven-day week) would be centered on the material for prayer applicable to each particular "week." The First Week seeks to bring the retreatant to a deeper under-standing of being a forgiven sinner through experiencing God's mercy and compassion. Various prayers, petitions, colloquies, and other suggestions accompany the main meditations. The Second Week focuses on the following of Christ and seeks to bring a person to a generous and magnanimous response to Christ's personal call. The retreatant is led to contemplate the mysteries of Christ's life so as to know him more intimately, to love him more ardently, and to follow him more closely. A key element in the Second Week is the election or choice of a state or way of life. The exercises of the Third Week are given to a contemplation of Christ's passion and death and the great love of God for us revealed in Christ's paschal mystery. The Fourth Week centers on Christ's glorious resurrec-tion. A key exercise in this final week is the *Contemplation to Attain the Love of God*, which brings out so clearly Ignatius's emphasis on "finding God in all things." In addition to the material for prayer pertinent to each week, the *Spiritual Exercises* include various methods of prayer, as well as a number of guidelines such as rules for the discernment of spirits, rules for thinking with the church, and rules for eating.

This brief description of the content of the *Exercises* should not leave one with the impression that the exercises are intended to achieve the same results for all who make them. They are meant to be flexible and adaptable to the particular needs of the individual retreatant. Although there is much material that is presented objectively, the retreatant is encouraged to be sensitive to the unique way God reveals himself, to be attentive to the interior movements of grace, and to follow the light and guidance of the Holy Spirit in prayer.

1. Introductory Material

"Soul of Christ"

The traditional prayer, *Anima Christi* (Soul of Christ), is usually printed at the beginning of the text of the *Spiritual Exercises*. This was a favorite prayer of Ignatius and he often recommends it explicitly as a prayer to be said by those making the exercises.[4] Although it was not included in the Spanish original or the early Latin editions, it later became the tradition to include it in all subsequent editions. The prayer does sum up the strong and ardent devotion of Christ that marks the *Spiritual Exercises*. The words of the prayer reflect this close identification with Christ that is to be sought by all who make the exercises:

> Soul of Christ, sanctify me. Body of Christ, save me. Blood of Christ, inebriate me. Water from the side of Christ, wash me. Passion of Christ, strengthen me. O good Jesus, hear me. Within your wounds hide me. Permit me not to be separated from you. From the malevolent enemy defend me. In the hour of my death call me, and bid me come to you, that with your saints I may praise you forever and ever. Amen.

The Annotations

Before proceeding to the exercises of the First Week, Ignatius makes a number of preliminary observations, intended mainly for the one who is giving the exercises. He presents these suggestions in the form of brief annotations or introductory explanations in order to aid the one giving the exercises and the one making them. He first seeks to clarify the meaning of the book's title.

> By the term Spiritual Exercises we mean every method of examination of conscience, meditation, contemplation, vocal or mental prayer, and other spiritual activities, such as will be mentioned later. For, just as taking a walk, traveling on foot, and running are physical exercises, so is the name of spiritual exercises given to any means of preparing and disposing our soul to rid itself of all its disordered affections and then, after their removal, of seeking and finding God's will in the ordering of our life for the salvation of our soul.[5]

Ignatius does expect the director to present material and suggestions for prayer but he also wants this to be done in a brief and summary manner. This is because those making the exercises will gain most through their own personal prayer and reflection that is enlightened by God's grace. As Ignatius puts it: "For, what fills and satisfies the soul consists, not in knowing much, but in our understanding the realities profoundly and in savoring them interiorly" (#2). Ignatius is also convinced that those making the exercises will benefit the most if they come to them with a spirit of generosity and magnanimity and a strong desire to do God's will. Among many other ways, this can be manifested by faithfully giving the full time to the various periods of prayer.

Ignatius also expects that in the course of their prayer, those making the exercises will experience various spiritual movements by way of personal responses. In general, he refers to these interior experiences as consolations and desolations, and he makes a number of suggestions so that the director can appropriately assist the retreatants according to their particular needs.[6] While giving the exercises, the director should also be careful not to unduly influence the retreatants as they seek to clarify God's will for themselves. Ignatius would want the director to take a more neutral stance if decisions are to be made so as "to allow the Creator to deal immediately with the creature and the creature with its Creator and Lord" (#15).

Finally, the flexibility of the exercises is highlighted (#18). They should be adapted to such variables as the age, education, health, and ability of those making them. For some, a shortened version may be more appropriate, while others may be ready to make the exercises in their entirety. Those who are able to disengage themselves from their ordinary pursuits and activities are encouraged to seek an atmosphere of solitude and seclusion so as to be more disposed to receive graces and gifts from the Divine Goodness (#20). However, the full exercises can be given in another form to those who cannot separate themselves from their daily occupations (#19).

At the end of these annotations or introductory observations, Ignatius has a brief but clear description of the purpose of the exercises. They are intended to remove any obstacles such as sin or disordered tendencies that would prevent persons from living according to God's plan for them. They also seek to bring those making the exercises to the point where they can make decisions in a manner that is free of any disordered affection. In Ignatius's own words the retreatant is "to overcome oneself and to order one's life without reaching a decision through some disordered affection" (#21).

2. The First Week

Principle and Foundation

Central to the First Week of the *Spiritual Exercises* is the rather brief but rich statement that comprises what is traditionally known as the *Principle and Foundation* (#23). Ignatius intends it to be carefully pondered and personally appropriated by the retreatant before moving on to the exercises that comprise the First Week. He was convinced that any subsequent spiritual growth and progress presupposed that the retreatant accepts in faith the foundational truths that are spelled out.

Summarizing much of Ignatius's worldview, it first speaks about the basic meaning of human existence. Human beings are created to praise, reverence, and serve God, and by means of this to save their souls. All other things on the face of the Earth have been created to help human beings reach their goal, and so all created things should be used or not used to the extent they further this end. There must be an essential link between what I choose and the end for which I have been created.

At this point, Ignatius introduces the concept of *indifference*, a term that plays a central role in his spirituality. It involves a basic stance of freedom vis-à-vis created things. It enables a person to be free of inordinate tendencies or biases that would prevent the making of wise and proper decisions. A spirit of indifference enables a person to desire and choose only the things that truly lead to the praise, reverence, and service of God and the end for which he or she has been created.

Meditations on Sin

The exercises of the First Week focus on what is traditionally known as the purgative way. Through a prayerful consideration of the history of sin and its consequences as well as one's own sinfulness, those making the exercises seek to come to a deeper realization of their personal sins and sinful tendencies, so that they can undergo a process of purification and thus turn more fully to God. In general, the material of this First Week is divided into two main divisions: first, various methods and suggestions for examining one's conscience (##24–44); second, a summary of the key exercises that Ignatius presents for the personal prayer of the retreatant (##45–72).

Ignatius himself, it will be recalled, always brought to his own spiritual life and prayer a strongly developed reflective process of self-examination. This is clearly reflected in the many methods and suggestions he makes for both the particular and general examination of conscience in the material for the First Week of the *Spiritual Exercises*. The instructions for the particular examination were concerned with overcoming a single sin or defect, while those for the general examination were primarily intended to assist the retreatant to make a general confession toward the end of the First Week.[7]

Ignatius proposes five key exercises for the prayer of the retreatants during the days of the First Week. He uses the term *meditation* for these early exercises, for at this stage he presupposes, given the subject matter, that the prayer of the retreatant will be of a more intellectual bent, marked by a good deal of reasoning and pondering. As a means to help one come to a deeper understanding of the spiritual realities that are proposed, he suggests that the mental powers of memory, understanding, and will be applied to the subject matter.

THE SPIRITUAL EXERCISES

Before proceeding to the actual subject matter, however, Ignatius offers some other helps to make the prayer more effective; he speaks of a preparatory prayer and two preludes. In the preparatory prayer the retreatant humbly turns to God and prays for the grace that whatever takes place during the period of prayer may be ordered completely to the service and praise of the Divine Majesty. The first prelude (usually referred to as the composition of place) is also intended to further a spirit of attention and greater focusing by bringing to the imagination the place or scene that is depicted in the material for prayer. The second prelude underscores the strong emphasis Ignatius places on the expressing of one's desires in prayer. The retreatant before each period of prayer is to ask God for what is wanted and desired in keeping with the subject matter. For example, in the mediation on personal sin, it will be to ask for a growing and intense sorrow and tears for one's sins.

Ignatius attaches great significance to the preparatory prayer and the two preludes because he was convinced that it was important to make a good beginning and to approach every period of prayer in a reverent and focused manner. For this reason they should be utilized at the beginning of every period of prayer throughout the course of the exercises. The preparatory prayer remains the same while the preludes can change according to the subject matter of the prayer.

The subject matter for the first meditation focuses on three individual sins: the sin of the angels; the sin of Adam and Eve; and the sin of anyone who has gone to hell because of one mortal sin. The retreatant is to apply his or her memory, understanding, and will to each of these sins, seeking to fathom the mystery of sin in the world and its far-reaching consequences, as well as recognizing one's own personal involvement.

To emphasize that this should not be merely an intellectual exercise but should involve the retreatant in a personal and subjective way, Ignatius introduces the important practice of the colloquy. This involves the retreatant in a prayerful conversation or dialogue with Christ, speaking with him from the heart. For this meditation retreatants are to place themselves before Christ on the cross, marveling at the love that is manifested there in the emptying of himself (kenosis) and the dying for our sins. Retreatants should then humbly ask themselves: "What have I done for Christ? What am I doing for Christ? What ought I to do for Christ?"

The second meditation follows the basic format of the previous one, although now the subject matter deals with one's *own* sins. Again, the retreatant is invited to apply the memory, understanding, and will to a review and a reflection of one's own sinfulness. The colloquy at the conclusion should be mindful of God's merciful love, and the retreatant is encouraged to give thanks for this mercy and resolve with God's grace to amend one's life.

In the third and fourth exercises, Ignatius introduces the important practice of the repetition, which will play a significant role during all the other exercises. In the third exercise the retreatant is to make a repetition of the first and second exercises, and in the fourth exercise to make a repetition of the third. In the repetitions, the ones making the exercises are not expected to approach the material in the same way as before, but to return to those aspects that moved or affected them personally. Ignatius expects God during the time of prayer to touch people in different ways with his grace, and so he wants the retreatants to grow in their sensitivity to these movements of grace. Thus, he urges them in the repetitions to notice and dwell on those points where they felt greater consolation or desolation or where they had a greater experience of God.

The fifth and final meditation of the First Week is on hell. Ignatius suggests that it be carried out by an application of the five senses to both the possibility and the reality of eternal damnation. Two of the benefits Ignatius hopes the retreatant might gain from this meditation are an added incentive to avoid sin in the future and an increasing gratitude for God's ongoing mercy and sustaining love. It should be noted here that although Ignatius himself does not provide any other material for the prayer of the First Week after this meditation, it has long been customary for the director of the exercises to suggest some other suitable material for prayer such as meditations on death, judgment, or the mercy of God manifested in such scriptural passages as the parable of the prodigal son (Luke 15:11–32).

Two points can be profitably highlighted before concluding this overview of the First Week. The first focuses on the importance of returning in prayer to those areas or movements where one has been particularly touched by God's grace. In one of the suggestions given at the end of the First Week (#76), Ignatius emphasizes that when individuals find what they are seeking, they should remain there until they are fully satisfied. In other words, there should be no anxiety about moving on too quickly to other points. It is far more helpful to remain and savor those aspects of prayer where one has been particularly helped and where one has found what is desired. This, of course, is linked with the importance Ignatius gives to the repetition during the days of prayer, for he does envisage one's prayer becoming more simplified and focused.

The second point has to deal with the growing sense of gratitude to God that Ignatius so highly values. In the colloquies of the later exercises of the First Week, this takes on an added importance, because Ignatius recognizes that this growing spirit of gratitude to God is a good sign that one is ready to move on to the exercises of the Second Week.

3. The Second Week

When the spiritual exercises are made in their full form of thirty days, retreatants normally devote the largest amount of time to the exercises of the Second Week. This is because Ignatius provides us with a great deal of significant material when he treats the Second Week. Here we only summarize his main points and leave to later chapters the development of some of the key issues.

The Call of Christ the King

The Second Week of the *Spiritual Exercises* is marked by a strong Christological thrust. Traditionally this emphasis has been called the "illuminative way" because it focuses on a devoted attachment and a generous following of Christ who is the "light of the world" (John 8:12). The exercise that introduces the Second Week clearly brings this out. Ignatius himself refers to this as the *Contemplation of the Kingdom of Jesus Christ*. Its purpose is to deepen that spirit of gratitude to Christ that developed in the First Week and to bring about now in the retreatants a strong desire to commit themselves generously to the person and service of the Lord. Ignatius suggests that they pray at the beginning of the exercise for the grace not to be deaf to Christ's call, but ready and diligent to accomplish his most holy will (#91).

The retreatant is led from a consideration of the call to the service of a temporal leader to the call of Christ the King. If the call of a good, brave, and charismatic human leader is worthy of a generous response, how much more is the call and invitation of Christ, Our Lord and eternal King. Those who are drawn in prayer to distinguish themselves in a total and generous service of Christ are invited to respond in an offering that culminates in the words: "I wish and desire, and it is my deliberate decision, provided only that it is for your greater service and praise, to imitate you in bearing all injuries and affronts, and any poverty, actual as well as spiritual, if your Most Holy Majesty desires to choose and receive me into such a life and state" (#98).

The Contemplations

The format of the exercises of the Second Week follows that which characterized the exercises of the First Week. Each exercise begins with the usual preparatory prayer and preludes, then develops the pertinent material for prayer by means of three points, and concludes with a colloquy. Again, it is expected that the prayer of the retreatant each day will grow more simplified and focused. New material for prayer is suggested for the first two exercises of prayer, while the last three periods of prayer are devoted to repetitions.

Although the general format is the same, the exercises of the Second Week take on a distinctly new focus. The person of Jesus Christ and the events that marked his earthly life now take the central place in the prayer of the retreatant. Traditionally these are referred to as the "mysteries of Christ." The third prelude (that moment before each period of prayer in which the retreatant asks for what is desired) takes on added importance in light of the Christological thrust of the Second Week. Now the retreatant is to ask for the grace "to have an interior knowledge of Our Lord, who became human for me, that I may love him more intensely and follow him more closely" (#104). It is a knowledge of the heart that is sought, a knowledge that leads to an ardent love of Christ and flowers in a dedicated and generous commitment to him.

The subject matter for the exercises of the first three days of the Second Week centers on the mystery of the incarnation, the birth of Jesus, and aspects of his hidden life. Later exercises will focus on the public life, beginning with Jesus' departure from Nazareth and his baptism by John the Baptist at the Jordan River, and followed by the temptations in the desert, the call of the apostles (Luke 3—5), and other familiar episodes (mysteries) as given to us in the Gospels. In all of these exercises the suggested method of prayer is what Ignatius calls *contemplation*. More will be said on this type of prayer when the various methods of Ignatian prayer are treated in a later chapter. Here only a general description is given.

Contemplation, as Ignatius envisages it, is a way of prayer in which the retreatant seeks to enter more deeply into a particular mystery in Christ's life. One pays careful attention in prayer to the persons, the words, and the actions that are depicted in a particular Gospel scene or passage. It is a form of gazing or viewing that seeks to draw the retreatant closer and closer to Christ. As a lover of art is drawn more and more into a particular painting by gazing intently upon it, even more so does Ignatius hope that a retreatant may be drawn closer and closer to Christ by contemplating various scenes from his life. David Fleming writes of Ignatian contemplation: "It is by means of this style of contemplative prayer that Ignatius has discovered a way of the retreatant imbibing Jesus' attitudes and approaches to God, to men and women, and to his world. The more we enter into gospel contemplation, the more we heighten the connaturality of our own way of living with the way that Christ lives."[8]

Special Exercises

In the midst of the contemplations of Christ's life, Ignatius inserts three special exercises during the course of the Second Week. He refers to them as the *Two Standards*, the *Three Classes of Persons*, and the *Three Ways (or Degrees) of Being Humble*. Their purpose is to assist further the retreatant who at this point may well be in the process of making a decision, particularly the choice of a state of life.

The meditation on the *Two Standards* takes place on the fourth day of the Second Week and focuses on a careful examination of the individual strategies of Christ and Lucifer. The retreatant is to pray for insight into the deceits of Lucifer (the mortal enemy of our human nature) and for the grace to guard against them, and then for insight into the way of Christ and for the grace to imitate him (#139).

The two ways or standards are clearly distinguished. The way of Lucifer seeks to lead a person from the coveting of riches to a desire for worldly honors, and then to a deeply rooted pride. From these ascending steps of riches, honor, and pride, one can then be led on to other vices. The way of Christ Our Lord counteracts each of these steps. It seeks to attract a person first to spiritual poverty and even *actual* poverty if it is God's will. It then seeks to lead a person to an attraction and desire to seek insults and the contempt of the world, for these lead to true humility. From these three steps of poverty, insults, and humility one can be led on to all other virtues.

A special colloquy consisting of three parts should follow this important meditation. Ignatius suggests that the retreatant approach Our Lady and ask her to obtain from her Son the grace to be received under his standard, ending with a "Hail Mary." The retreatant should then ask for the same grace from the Son that he might obtain it from the Father, closing with the prayer, *Anima Christi* (Soul of Christ). Finally, this request is made directly to God the Father and closes with the saying of the "Our Father" (#147).

The meditation on the *Three Classes* immediately follows that of the *Two Standards*. Ignatius realizes that knowledge and insights about the standard and values of Christ must also be accompanied by a readiness and freedom of the will. Thus he introduces a meditation that sheds light on the varying degrees of freedom individuals can bring to an actual decision. This mediation focuses on three persons, each representing a certain class of people. Each person has to make a decision about the proper use of a sum of money, but each approaches it with different degrees of openness and readiness of the will. The first two are greatly limited in their ability to choose and act because of previous attachments and attitudes. It is only the person of the third class who is free enough of these attachments to choose that which is most pleasing to God and the salvation of one's soul. This meditation also ends with the same three colloquies that concluded the meditation of the *Two Standards*.

Ignatius introduces the third special exercise at the point where the retreatant is considering an election or a choice of life. He refers to it as the *Three Ways of Humility* and he presents it as a consideration, similar to the *Principle and Foundation* of the First Week. The material given for this exercise in ##165–68 is to be pondered prayerfully from time to time while one is engaged in decision making. Its purpose is to bring the retreatant to a loving desire to be identified with Christ as closely as possible. It seeks to stir up a spirit of generosity and magnanimity that flows from a loving relationship with Christ. It treats the three ways or manners of being lovingly humble.[9]

Ignatius presents these three ways of being humble in a sequence that becomes increasingly deeper. The first way is marked by a desire to be so obedient to the law of God that under no circumstance would one want to violate a commandment that binds under mortal sin. The second way is more perfect. It is characterized not only by the spirit of freedom and indifference that the *Principle and Foundation* speaks about, but also by the conviction that "neither for all creation nor to save my life would I ever reach a decision to commit a venial sin" (#166). The third way is the most perfect. It presupposes the first two but goes on to involve a person in a loving desire to be as closely identified with Christ as possible. It leads a person to desire poverty with Christ rather than wealth; contempt with Christ rather than honors; and even a desire to be regarded as a fool for Christ rather than as a wise or prudent person. It is the attitude that would lead a person to proclaim: "I love Christ and want to be as like to him as possible, no matter what the cost."[10]

Since Ignatius considers this such a significant exercise, he again suggests that the retreatant make the triple colloquy that was mentioned earlier (#47). If one is drawn to the third way of being humble, he or she should beg for the grace to be chosen for this closer way of imitating and serving the Lord—provided of course that it be for the service and praise of the Divine Majesty.

The Election

Ignatius attaches great importance to making a well-ordered decision, or "election," about one's life during the course of the exercises of the Second Week. For some, the election might focus on choosing a particular state of life, while for others who have already chosen their state of life, it may be seeking to increase the spiritual quality of that life. As a means of assisting the retreatant to make as enlightened a decision as possible, he offers a number of suggestions concerning this process in ##169–89 of the *Exercises*. Only some of his key points will be mentioned here.

Ignatius first emphasizes that all decisions should be made in light of our final end. That end, as the *Principle and Foundation* of the First Week teaches, is the praise, reverence, and service of God and the salvation of one's soul. Thus, anything chosen should be a means or an aid to achieve that goal. In other words, the means should be ordered to the end, and not the other way around. Our aim at all times must be the service and praise of God; any decision or choice should only be made in light of this aim.

For Ignatius, there are three suitable "times" for making a sound and good election or decision. The first time occurs when God so moves and attracts the will of a person that there is no doubt that this is God's will. As examples of this type, Ignatius speaks of the direct calling of Saint Paul and Saint Matthew. The second time occurs when sufficient clarity and knowledge emerge from the experiences of consolation and desolation during the time of prayer and the discernment of the various spirits. More will be said of this important process of discernment in a later chapter. The third time (referred to as a "time of tranquility") takes place apart from any movements of the various spirits; during this time retreatants use their natural faculties, particularly the intellect, to consider a decision in freedom and peace.

Ignatius goes on to suggest two ways of proceeding in the third time. The first calls for retreatants to put before themselves the matter about which they wish to make a decision. After praying for God's guidance and assistance and disposing themselves to seek God's will apart from any disordered affections, retreatants are to ponder calmly and to weigh carefully the advantages and disadvantages, the pros and cons, connected with each aspect of the decision. When this reasoning has been completed and a decision has been reached, the retreatants are to bring it to God in prayer so that it may be received and confirmed.

The second way in this third time includes some further suggestions that entail a greater use of the imagination. In one instance retreatants would imagine what advice they would give to a stranger, having only in mind what would be best for his or her eternal salvation and the greater glory of God. In another instance they would picture themselves on their deathbed and consider the present decision from that viewpoint and perspective. In a final example given by Ignatius, they imagine themselves on judgment day and consider the decision from that critical moment. Each one of these cases can assist the retreatant to see the present decision in a much larger perspective.

Ignatius concludes this section on the election with some suggestions "for amending and reforming one's own life and state" (#189). He has in mind in this section those who are established in their own vocation in life but wish to continue the important process of spiritual renewal and growth. This would be the case for many who make an annual retreat.

4. The Third and Fourth Weeks

There is a twofold purpose for the exercises of the Third and Fourth Weeks. There is first of all the aspect of confirmation. The exercises now seek to strengthen and confirm retreatants in their preceding prayer and decisions by contemplating the sufferings and death of Christ during the Third Week and the joy of the Risen Christ during the Fourth Week. But there is also a unitive aspect, for they seek to bring about a closer and more intimate association with Christ in his paschal mystery. There is to be a fuller and deeper response to the call of Christ the King on the part of the retreatant by uniting with Christ in the sufferings of his passion and death and the joy and glory of his resurrection.

The exercises of the Third Week focus on the passion and death of Christ, beginning with the events of the Last Supper and concluding with his death on the cross. Contemplation is the preferred method of prayer and the repetitions and colloquies are to have a central place in the prayer of the retreatant. The grace that is to be sought is "sorrow, regret, and confusion, because the Lord is going to his Passion for my sins" (#193). One is to be with Christ in his suffering and sorrow, sharing interiorly in "the great suffering which Christ endured for me." The growing realization that Christ suffered for my sins should lead me to ask: "What ought I to do and suffer for him?" (#197).

The subject matter of the Fourth Week centers on the mysteries of Christ's resurrection up to and including the ascension. Throughout this week retreatants are to contemplate the appearances of the Risen Christ to those who were close to him in life, beginning with an appearance to his Blessed Mother. What is desired now in prayer is "the grace to be glad and to rejoice intensely because of the great glory and joy of Christ our Lord" (#221). Those who shared in the sorrow and shame of the passion during the Third Week are now invited to an intimate association with the Risen Christ in his glory and joy and to share in a particular way in the strengthening consolation and peace he brought to those to whom he appeared. The exercises of the Fourth Week are associated with what is traditionally known as the "unitive way," for they seek to bring about a deeper and more profound union with Christ.

Contemplation to Attain Love

Central to the union with Christ that marks the Fourth Week is the celebrated exercise that Ignatius calls the *Contemplation to Attain Love*. It is an exercise that can either be prayed in connection with the other mysteries of the Fourth Week or made as the final exercise of the retreat. It is a contemplation that serves as a fitting climax to all the seeking of God that has taken place in the preceding weeks of prayer. But it also serves as a transition to the future, for it is hoped that retreatants will continue the process of seeking to be united with God in their daily lives and finding God in all things.

This contemplation seeks simply and directly to increase one's love for God. As the second prelude puts it so well, the retreatant desires now "to ask for interior knowledge of all the great good I have received, in order that, stirred to profound gratitude, I may become able to love and serve the Divine Majesty in all things" (#233).

Ignatius begins this contemplation with two practical observations. First, he reminds us that love expresses itself more by deeds than by words; actions indeed speak louder than words. Second, retreatants should keep in mind that love consists of a mutual sharing between two persons. A person who loves wishes to give and share with the beloved what he or she possesses.

Ignatius then asks the retreatants to reflect on God's love for them from different perspectives. For example, retreatants are first to recall and ponder in prayer the gifts they have received from the hand of God, both the gifts of creation and redemption that are shared by all and the special gifts that are unique to their own lives. The awareness of these gifts and the realization that the same God desires to share his very self can only lead to a profound spirit of gratitude and a deep desire to love in return.

The concluding prayer that Ignatius suggests after these reflections as well as the other points he offers to deepen the awareness of God's love is one of the most familiar ones associated with him. The retreatant should pray with deep love and affection:

> Take, Lord, and receive all my liberty, my memory, my understanding, and all my will—all that I have and possess. You, Lord, have given all that to me. I now give it back to you, O Lord. All of it is yours. Dispose of it according to your will. Give me your love and grace, for that is enough for me. (#234)

Conclusion

The one who made these spiritual exercises now goes forth to take up again the regular occupations of everyday life. But it is not intended to be the end. Ignatius certainly would hope that the vision of the world and one's own life would be different. His prayer would be that the one who made the exercises might now continue the process of finding God in all things and seeking above all the praise and service of the Divine Majesty in all the actions of one's life.

4

IGNATIAN PRAYER

Ignatius had no intention of writing a systematic study of prayer in the *Spiritual Exercises*, but he does bring to the attention of the retreatants a number of different ways of approaching God in prayer. These were primarily aimed at assisting people during the time they were actually making the exercises. The benefit gained and the facility acquired during the days of making the exercises could easily extend to one's prayer in the future. Thus, broadly speaking, we can refer to the exercises as a "school for prayer."

When the term *Ignatian prayer* is used, it normally refers to the various methods or ways of prayer Ignatius teaches and explains in the pages of the *Spiritual Exercises*. It is important to keep in mind that methods of prayer did not begin with Ignatius. He was heir to those aspects of medieval piety and devotion that were taught by members of the Benedictine, Cistercian, Franciscan, and Victorine schools, as well as those connected with the *Devotio Moderna* movement of the fourteenth century. It will also be recalled that during his recuperation from battle wounds Ignatius was greatly influenced by two well-known medieval writings, *The Life of Christ* by the Carthusian, Ludolph of Saxony, and the popular lives of the saints known as *The Golden Legend* by a thirteenth-century Dominican, Jacopo de Voragine. He also came into contact with other aspects of Benedictine and Dominican piety during his days at Montserrat and Manresa after his conversion. Ignatius did much to popularize the teachings on prayer that he inherited from these various sources by presenting and teaching them in a much more simplified and practical way that proved to be very effective. His teaching in turn greatly influenced many spiritual writers and masters of the spiritual life who came after him.

This chapter looks more carefully at these Ignatian methods that have been so helpful to many in their seeking of God in prayer.[1] Some preliminaries are presented first.

1. Preparation for Prayer

Throughout the *Spiritual Exercises*, Saint Ignatius seeks to maintain that delicate balance and tension between God's grace and human activity. Prayer in his mind involves both personal activity and surrender to the inspirations of the Holy Spirit. He realized that there could be no real prayer without the grace of God being active at every stage. The role of the Holy Spirit is central and prayer is essentially the activity of the Holy Spirit within us. Ignatius was no less aware of our need to cooperate with God's grace with an ongoing spirit of attentiveness, generosity, and docility. This docility manifests itself in the attitudes and dispositions that a person brings to prayer and the steps taken to prepare oneself. Thus, we should not be surprised that Ignatius emphasizes certain dispositions for prayer and various means of preparation.

First, Ignatius emphasizes a spirit of generosity and magnanimity. We recall his words at the beginning of the *Exercises*: "The persons who make the Exercises will benefit greatly by entering upon them with great spirit and generosity toward their Creator and Lord, and by offering all their desires and freedom to him so that His Divine Majesty can make use of their persons and of all they possess in whatsoever way is in accord with his most holy will" (#5). Here he echoes those familiar words of Saint Paul: "He who sows sparingly will reap sparingly, and he who sows bountifully will reap bountifully" (2 Cor 9:6). Ignatius wants this spirit of generosity to be present at every stage of the prayer, particularly when the prayer seems unproductive. For example, if a person is tempted to shorten the allotted time of prayer during times of desolation and dryness, Ignatius suggests that this be countered by extending a little the allotted time. He calls for a generosity that costs.

Closely connected with this generosity for Ignatius is a spirit of self-abnegation or detachment. This is the indifference that the *Principle and Foundation* speaks about at the beginning of the *Spiritual Exercises*. It is not an end in itself but a means to keep oneself free from disordered affections or attachments that prevent a person from being focused on God or attuned to his divine will. Only a free person can fully seek and embrace the will of God. But this freedom does not happen in any automatic way. It calls for an ongoing spirit of sacrifice, generosity, and attentiveness to the direction of one's deepest desires. This is why Ignatius attaches such importance to the daily examinations of conscience. If the heart is divided, it is impossible to maintain that purity of heart that is essential for a deep union with God.

Ignatius was convinced that it was important to make a good beginning and approach *every* period of prayer in a reverent and focused manner. Thus, he strongly recommends some preparatory steps before each exercise of prayer. One should first consciously place oneself in the presence of God. As Ignatius writes: "A step or two away from the place where I will make my contemplation or meditation, I will stand for the length of an Our Father. I will raise my mind and think how God our Lord is looking at me, and other such thoughts. Then I will make an act of reverence or humility" (#75). This is followed by a preparatory prayer that seeks God's help, asking "for the grace that all my intentions, actions, and operations may be ordered purely to the service and praise of the Divine

Majesty" (#46). He suggests that this same preparatory prayer be used at the beginning of every meditation or contemplation.

What Ignatius refers to as "preludes "are also suggested as part of the preparation, for they are intended to aid us in disposing ourselves for prayer. The suggested use of the preludes will vary according to the subject matter but there are two that Ignatius recommends for *all* of the exercises of meditation or contemplation. The first, referred to as the "composition of place," makes use of the imagination to recall briefly the place or scene that is spoken about in the matter for prayer. The second focuses on the particular grace that is sought according to the subject matter. I am to ask God Our Lord for that which I wish and desire. For example, if the contemplation is on the resurrection, I should ask for joy with Christ rejoicing. Or while contemplating the mysteries of Christ's life during the Second Week, I ask for an interior knowledge of Our Lord, that I may the more love him and follow him. This prelude focuses on the *id quod volo* (that which I desire), a term that is repeated many times in the *Exercises* when Ignatius suggests this prelude.

Let us now turn to the various methods or different ways of prayer that Ignatius teaches in the pages of the *Spiritual Exercises*. The three major methods are what he calls meditation, contemplation, and the application of senses. But there are a number of other methods that will also be treated in the following pages after examining the three major ones. It always has to be kept in mind, of course (and this is something Ignatius realized so well), that the Holy Spirit is *the* great teacher of prayer and that any methods that are suggested by human authors are only intended as means to help a person in the process of being attentive and responsive to the movements of the Holy Spirit.

2. Meditation

Meditation is the first method of prayer Ignatius speaks about in the *Spiritual Exercises*. He refers to it as "meditation by using the three powers of the soul" (#45).[2] Again, Ignatius is very much in the current of earlier Western spirituality when he makes use of this method that applies the memory, understanding, and will to a particular teaching of the faith, or to some text from Scripture or the Liturgy, or to some event in Christ's life. This is the form of prayer he suggests for the early exercises of the First Week when the material proposed for prayer focuses on such themes as the historical dimensions of sin, one's personal sinfulness, and the consideration of hell. It is the method he also suggests for such exercises of the Second Week as the *Two Standards* and the *Three Classes of Persons*. It is usually referred to as discursive prayer, for it does give a prominent role to intellectual pondering. It is also a method that is particularly helpful for those who are at an early stage of spiritual growth.

The memory is employed at the beginning of the prayer. It brings to mind the particular subject matter that has been suggested by a director or the material that one has previously read. The intellect or understanding then begins the work of reflecting on, breaking up, and pondering this material so that it can be made one's own and personally and more easily assimilated. But Ignatius brings out a special word of caution in one of his preliminary observations in the *Exercises*: it is not a question of covering a lot of material or trying to understand many things in an abstract way, "for what fills and satisfies the soul consists, not in knowing much, but in our understanding the realities profoundly and in savoring them interiorly" (#2). It is an interior knowledge and understanding that Ignatius has in mind that goes far beyond mere speculative knowledge. Speaking of this interior knowledge that is sought in meditation, Father Brou writes: "There is in this much more than a speculative grasp of the truth. It is warm, practical, experimental, personal, truly interior. We not only see, we *realize*."³

When one begins under God's grace to understand these realities of faith and to savor them interiorly, the third power of the soul, the will, plays a more prominent role. The acts that are proper to the will are usually designated by the terms *affections* and *resolutions*. When the will is involved, the prayer becomes more affective. Affections are those responses and movements that arise in the will as a result of the activity of the intellect. These would include such responses as acts of faith, hope, and love, acts of petition, expressions of praise, thanksgiving, sorrow for sin, and trust in God. They are the impulses or movements of the soul to God. These various affections, however, do not exhaust the role of the will in prayer, for one's prayer should also take on a practical dimension. Appropriate resolutions made by the will look to the future and one's daily life and can provide a solid way of enhancing one's relationship with God.

As is the case with his other methods of prayer, Ignatius wants the colloquy to have a central role in a meditation according to the three powers of the soul. One should not end the meditation without first speaking directly to God. A colloquy involves a person in a simple and direct turning to God or Christ in prayer. As Ignatius himself describes it at the end of the first exercise of the First Week, "a colloquy is made, properly speaking, in the way one friend speaks to another, or a servant to one in authority—now begging a favor, now accusing oneself of some misdeed, now telling one's concerns and asking counsel about them" (#54).

Thus, although the method of meditation may seem somewhat complicated and more discursive at first glance, it does indeed follow a process that is intended to become more and more simplified. It is necessary to bring wood to the fire but it is the fire itself that is important. Love has a way of simplifying things, and God's grace "has a tendency to bring all interior operations to unity. As the soul progresses it gets rid of all that is complex and multiple."[4] Once again Ignatius's advice should be recalled: when you find in prayer what is nourishing, do not be in any hurry to go on; stay and relish what is given by the Lord. For it is not an abundance of words and ideas that satisfies the soul, but "the interior and practical taste of the things meditated."[5] Finally, the key role that Ignatius gives to the exercises of repetition as a means of simplifying and deepening one's prayer should be kept in mind. The repetitions are intended to help a person become more sensitive to the individual movements of God's grace by returning in prayer to those aspects that were particularly fruitful and helpful.

3. Contemplation

Contemplation is the second way of praying that Ignatius teaches in the *Spiritual Exercises*. (It should be noted here at the beginning that he is using the term *contemplation* in a somewhat different way from what later writers on mystical theology will call acquired contemplation and infused contemplation.) He introduces it early in the Second Week when the subject matter for prayer begins to focus on events (traditionally referred to as "mysteries") in the life of the historical Jesus.[6] It will go on to become Ignatius's preferred way of praying during the Second, Third, and Fourth Weeks of the *Spiritual Exercises*. It tends to be a more simplified form of prayer than meditation, for it is mainly a way of looking at and focusing carefully on a particular episode as given to us in the Gospels. In contemplation, the retreatant seeks to relive the Gospel mystery and become part of it through a personal engagement with the persons, words, and actions. It is more an affective than discursive way of praying, for it seeks primarily to unite us with Christ in a tender and heartfelt way.

This tender and devout reflection on the human aspects of the life of Christ, especially his passion and death on the cross, became very popular during the last centuries of the Middle Ages, particularly the thirteenth and fourteenth. It was widely developed by writers in the Franciscan school, as well as proponents of the *Devotio Moderna* and spiritual writers from the ranks of the Benedictines, Cistercians, Carthusians, and Dominicans. Ignatius most likely made contact with this tradition for the first time when he read the *Life of Christ* by the Carthusian, Ludolph of Saxony, while recuperating at Loyola at the time of his conversion. This initial contact was no doubt nourished and deepened during his days at Montserrat and Manresa. Thus, Ignatius was very much part of an earlier tradition of prayer when he developed the method he called *contemplation* in the *Spiritual Exercises*. He simplified it somewhat by structuring the details of a particular contemplation on the life of Christ around a threefold division: persons, words, and actions.

Let us turn now to Ignatius's own directions and suggestions for this way of prayer as given to us for the contemplation on Our Lord's nativity at the beginning of the Second Week of the *Exercises*. After noting the usual preparatory steps and the preludes of briefly recalling the pertinent historical facts, imaging the place, and asking for what is desired, Ignatius develops the following three points that focus on persons, words, and actions. He writes:

> *The First Point*. This is to see the persons; that is, to see Our Lady, Joseph, the maidservant, and the infant Jesus after his birth. I will make myself a poor, little, and unworthy slave, gazing at them, contemplating them, and serving them in their needs, just as if I were there with all possible respect and reverence. Then I will reflect upon myself to draw some profit.

The Second Point. I will observe, consider, and contemplate what they are saying. Then, reflecting upon myself, I will draw some profit.

The Third Point. This is to behold and consider what they are doing; for example, journeying and toiling, in order that the Lord may be born in greatest poverty; and that after so many hardships of hunger, thirst, heat, cold, injuries, and insults, he may die on the cross! And all this for me! Then I will reflect and draw some spiritual profit.

Colloquy. Conclude with a colloquy, as in the preceding contemplation, and with an Our Father. (##110–17)

Some brief observations on these words may be helpful. First, although the focus here is on the birth of Jesus at Bethlehem, it is a way of praying that can be used for *all* the mysteries connected with his hidden and public life. It is not so much a question of reflecting and analyzing a particular mystery as it is of being a part of it. We seek to relive the mystery in our own way and in our own hearts. We are urged to bring the mystery before us in a personal way, to insert ourselves into it, to "see the persons," "to observe, consider what they are saying," "to behold and consider what they are doing." This in turn should lead the heart to respond with various affections—with respect and reverence, with love, with sorrow, with praise, with holy desires and resolutions. Finally, there should also be some practical applications to one's own life. At the end of each one of the above points, Ignatius urges us "to reflect upon ourselves and to draw some profit."

Foremost among this spiritual profit should be a deepening union and personal commitment to the person of Jesus Christ. Ignatius brings this out clearly when he suggests that in all the exercises involving contemplations on the life of Jesus during the Second Week, the grace that should be sought is "to have an interior knowledge of Our Lord, who became human for me, that I may love him more intensely and follow him more closely" (#104). Again, as was the case for meditation using the three powers of the soul, the knowledge that is sought in contemplation is not an abstract or speculative knowledge, but an *interior* one. It is a knowledge that comes from a faith-filled and loving heart. It is a knowledge that springs from love and leads to a deeper, more ardent, and total love of Christ, Our Lord. Finally, it is an interior knowledge and love that leads a person to respond more generously to the call of Christ as articulated in the kingdom meditation, "Come, follow me, come, labor with me."

4. Application of the Senses

Ignatius introduces the method of prayer that he calls the "application of the senses" in connection with the contemplation on the nativity early in the Second Week of the *Exercises*.[7] Like the previous two methods, this, too, was taught by spiritual writers of the Middle Ages. Ignatius, however, develops it in a precise way and suggests that it be used at a particular time of prayer. It will be recalled that when the spiritual exercises are made in their entirety, there are ordinarily five periods of prayer for each day. The method Ignatius refers to as the "application of the senses" is to be used for the fifth and final period of prayer that is made in the evening. Thus, it is intended as a means of developing and deepening in a somewhat quiet and less active way the fruit that was gained in the previous contemplations of the day.

Ignatius writes that after the preparatory prayer and the preludes, "it is profitable to use the imagination and to apply the five senses to the first and second contemplation" (i.e., the incarnation and the nativity). He goes on to outline this method in the following points.

> *The First Point*. By the sight of my imagination I will see the persons, by meditating and contemplating in detail all the circumstances around them, and by drawing some profit from the sight.

> *The Second Point*. By my hearing I will listen to what they are saying or might be saying: and then, reflecting on myself, I will draw some profit from this.

> *The Third Point*. I will smell the fragrance and taste the infinite sweetness and charm of the Divinity, of the soul, of its virtues, and everything there, appropriately for each of the persons who is being contemplated. Then I will reflect upon myself and draw profit from this.

> *The Fourth Point*. Using the sense of touch, I will, so to speak, embrace and kiss the places where the persons walk or sit. I shall always endeavor to draw some profit from this.

> *Colloquy*. Conclude with a colloquy as in the first and second contemplations, and with an Our Father. (##121–26)

The imagination has a key role in this method of prayer and Ignatius is clearly presenting us with a formula for imaginative prayer. It is interesting to note, however, that *unlike* the previous two forms of prayer, this one has given rise to different interpretations. Frankly, some have not regarded it too highly, considering it inferior to meditation and contemplation because it is an exercise of a "lower" faculty, the imagination. They would see it more suited for beginners and a good method for times of fatigue. Others actually consider it superior to meditation and contemplation and a method that can lead to what many spiritual writers refer to as "acquired contemplation." This is because they see it as an application of Saint Bonaventure's teaching on the "spiritual senses" as developed in his great medieval work, *The Soul's Journey into God*.[8]

Recent writers on Ignatian prayer have tended to favor the second interpretation—and there is much in Ignatius's own account that would support it. After speaking in the first two points of seeing and hearing with the imagination, Ignatius goes much deeper in the third point, using language that calls to mind the spiritual senses. We "will smell the fragrance and taste the infinite sweetness and charm of the Divinity." It is a prayer that echoes the words of the Psalmist: "O taste and see that the LORD is good" (Ps 34:8). It is a prayer of the heart that seeks to assimilate the fruit that has been gained from the earlier prayer of the day and to continue the process of "reflecting on myself and drawing some profit."

5. Three Additional Methods

The three methods of prayer we have been discussing—meditation, contemplation, and application of the senses—are the principal ones that Ignatius develops in the pages of the *Spiritual Exercises*. But they are certainly not the only ones. In the supplementary material found immediately after the Fourth Week (##238–60), Ignatius teaches three additional methods, all quite practical, helpful, and uncomplicated in their format. Although they can be used with profit by all, both beginners and those more advanced, Ignatius especially recommended them for those who could not make the exercises in their entirety.[9]

The subject matter for the first of these three methods focuses on such themes as the Ten Commandments, the seven capital sins and their opposite virtues, and the correct use of one's faculties and the five senses of the body. In the first example that he entitles "On the Ten Commandments," Ignatius recommends that a preparatory prayer be made first in which one asks for God's help that "I may be able to know how I have failed against the ten commandments. Similarly I will ask for grace and aid to amend myself for the future" (#240). A person will then reflect on the first commandment for a brief time (about the time it would take to recite three "Our Fathers" and three "Hail Marys," although this can vary for individual needs), reflecting on how this commandment has been observed. If one discovers any failures, God's forgiveness and pardon will be sought and an "Our Father" will be recited. This same procedure will continue for each of the Ten Commandments. After the examination of all the commandments is made, one should acknowledge one's failures, seek God's pardon, and resolve to make amends before concluding with a colloquy.

In addition to the areas that Ignatius explicitly mentions as examples, this method can be extended with some minor adaptations to other areas of the Christian life, such as the virtues, the Beatitudes, the gifts of the Holy Spirit, religious vows, and retreat resolutions, to name a few examples. Resembling in many aspects the general examen of conscience, this method of prayer can provide ongoing assistance for growth in Christian living and for perseverance in one's retreat resolutions and other good intentions during the course of daily living.

The second method of praying, the text of the *Spiritual Exercises* goes on to tell us, "consists in contemplating each word of a prayer." It is a type of prayer that is very much in the revered Benedictine tradition of *lectio divina*, the prayerful reading and assimilation of scriptural texts and other devotional reading. Ignatius's particular focus in this second method of prayer, however, is on traditional *prayers* rather than *texts*. For example, a person can choose the "Our Father" and say the word *Father* and then proceed to ponder that word carefully in one's heart, seeking to draw nourishment, understanding, and consolation from its meaning and reality. The individual word should be considered as long as profit can be gained, for the goal is not to hurry on to complete the prayer, but to savor and relish the significance of each individual word. Thus, the same procedure should be followed with each word of the prayer. It is suggested that a person spend an hour considering the prayer in this manner, but there is no need to finish the prayer itself. The one praying can spend the whole hour on a few words if they yield relish and consolation. In this case the rest of the prayer can be recited at the end of the hour in the customary way.

This method of prayer can be used, of course, for other prayers such as the "Hail Mary," *Animi Christi*, the Creed, various psalms, canticles, and hymns, as well as prayers that are part of the Eucharistic Liturgy or Liturgy of the Hours. Ignatius adds as a note that when a person finishes a particular prayer in the manner described, one should then turn to the person to whom the prayer has been directed and ask for the virtues or graces that are particularly needed.

There are certain benefits that can flow from this type of prayer. It can certainly lead a person to a deeper understanding and appreciation of a particular prayer and to a greater affinity with it. It can do much to overcome the familiarity and sense of routine that can arise from the frequent recitation and use of a certain prayer. It can help a person pray with greater devotion and attention the prayers of the Divine Office or the prayers of the eucharistic canon, and other hymns, canticles, and sequences. Finally, prayers that have been deeply assimilated and internalized can sustain a person and make prayer possible in more difficult external circumstances, such as illness, fatigue, or a noisy or distracting atmosphere.

The third method of prayer Ignatius teaches in this group of three is a form of "rhythmic" prayer. He describes it as "praying according to rhythmic measures" (#258). Like the preceding second method, it takes as its subject a particular prayer. The prayer is recited interiorly in a slow, rhythmic way in which a word is pronounced with each breath. Between each breath one can reflect on the meaning of the word, or on the person to whom the prayer is being directed. Less mental activity is required with this method than with the previous two, so it may be used with profit when a person is in the midst of distracting work, or when tired, or when traveling.

Whereas the second method of prayer is in the Benedictine tradition of *lectio divina*, this method has more in common with the rhythmic tradition of the Jesus Prayer that has long been popular in the spirituality of the Eastern Church. In this prayer, a formula such as "Lord, Jesus Christ, Son of the Living God, have mercy on me a sinner" is recited with each breath in order to bring about a deepening union with God.[10]

6. The General Examen

Ignatius gives us the format for making the general examination of conscience early in the pages of the *Spiritual Exercises* (#43). He always attached great importance and significance to this way of prayer, for he saw it as a graced opportunity for a person to take stock of his or her relationship with God at a fixed time each day.

There has been a renewed appreciation of the general examen in recent times.[11] It is an appreciation that links the examen with the process of discernment and thus looks upon it more as an examen of *consciousness* rather than only an examen of conscience. It is more commonly known today as the "awareness examen." Its main purpose is to help us become more aware of God's activity in our daily lives and more sensitive to the many ways God touches us. Thus, it is an important way of seeking and finding God in all things and responding more fully to his loving call.

The format that Ignatius suggests for this form of daily prayer (normally made at the close of the day) involves five steps. The first step is to recall any graces and blessing that have been received that day and then give thanks to God for them. An ongoing sense of gratitude can do much to open our hearts more fully to the power of God working in our lives. The second step is to pray for light and for greater insight into the way God has been present to me during the day and the ways I have or have not responded to him. In the third step a prayerful review of the day is made. I first seek to become more aware of God's action within me, of the interior movements that may have arisen in me during the course of the day, both the ones that seemed to draw me to God and the ones that drew me away from him. In other words, I seek to discern and clarify how God has been present to me during the day. Then I reflect on my responses and my actions—the times I have responded to his graces and the times I have failed to do so. In the last two steps, I acknowledge my faults and failings and humbly seek God's forgiveness, and then resolve with his grace to do better and to go on with renewed hope and trust.

Conclusion

As we conclude this survey of the various ways or methods that are associated with Ignatian prayer, it should be kept in mind that they are intended as *aids* for prayer. In no way are they ends in themselves. No one should ever feel constrained by any particular way of praying, and various methods should be used only insofar as they help us to find God in our prayer. There should always be a spirit of freedom connected with prayer, for it is the Holy Spirit that leads individuals to pray in the way best suited for them. Prayer is essentially the activity of the Holy Spirit within us and methods are only a means to help a person in the process of being attentive to the movements of the Holy Spirit. As Ignatius was fond of pointing out in the *Constitutions*, a person's prayer should be guided by a discerning love.

It should also be emphasized once again that Ignatian prayer is marked by an outward thrust. Ignatius always wanted prayer to be integrated with one's work and daily activities, and he was constantly encouraging others to meet the challenge of harmonizing their work and their prayer. For example, in a letter to his close Jesuit collaborator, Jerome Nadal, Ignatius writes: "Our prayer should be such that it increases in us the spiritual taste for labor…and the labor should increase virtue and delight in prayer."[12]

This integration of prayer and the rest of life is summed up in the familiar Ignatian phrases "finding God in all things" and being a "contemplative in action." The desire to seek and find God in all things and to embrace his will with generosity was always foremost in Ignatius's mind. That is why he always valued so highly the daily examen of conscience (consciousness). It is the reason, too, for his placing that key prayer, the *Contemplation to Attain Love*, right at the end of the *Spiritual Exercises*. One's prayer should lead to an ever-growing sensitivity to the many ways God moves and acts in our lives.

This capacity to be sensitive to God's presence in one's daily life calls for a discerning heart. It is to this subject of Ignatian discernment that we turn in the following chapter.

5

IGNATIAN DISCERNMENT

As is the case with other aspects of Ignatian spirituality, the topic of discernment is not original to Ignatius. It has deep roots in Scripture and it has a long and valued place in the history of Christian spirituality. John Cassian, Saint Bonaventure, Saint Thomas Aquinas, John Gerson, and many others have all made significant contributions in this area.[1] The process of discernment for Ignatius, however, was central in his life and apostolic vision, and the contributions and insights that have emerged from his writings, particularly the *Spiritual Exercises*, have had a widespread and lasting influence. The desire to seek and find God in all things and to embrace his will with generosity was the driving force in Ignatius's life from the time of his conversion. He also developed the spiritual exercises as a means to assist others to order their lives in such a way that they would have the freedom and desire to find and embrace God's will in their individual lives. Thus, discernment is an integral part of Ignatian spirituality.

Some general reflections on discernment may be helpful at this point. First, discernment should *not* be considered a cause or an issue or even a method in itself. Basically, discernment is a *process* in prayer by which one seeks seriously to know and follow God's will, to hear his call, and to respond faithfully and generously in the very real-life situation of the person concerned. As John Futrell writes, discernment "involves choosing the way of the light of Christ instead of the way of the darkness of the Evil One and living out the consequences of this choice through discerning what specific decisions and actions are demanded to follow Christ here and now."[2] Thus, discernment focuses on the ongoing attempts to clarify and ascertain God's will in our lives and seeks to specify what actions and decisions are required in the life of one who wishes to follow Christ totally. At the heart of this process is a spirit of prayer, for the context of any true discernment is one's ongoing prayer and a desire to be united with God.

The brief treatment of Ignatian discernment presented in this chapter focuses first on the process of discernment in Ignatius's own life. Second, it recalls some of the main insights and aspects of his teaching that are contained in the *Spiritual Exercises*. It concludes with some thoughts on the importance of seeking to discern and find God's presence in the course of daily living.

1. Discernment in Ignatius's Life

Ignatius's *Autobiography* is the best source for seeing the ongoing development and growth in the process of discernment that took place in his spiritual journey.[3] He sought to present in this memoir an account of his growing awareness of God's action in his life and the slow but steady growth that took place in his capacity to recognize the authentic movements of God. The process began seriously while he was recuperating from his wounds at Loyola, a period that found him awakening to the grace of God that was working powerfully in his life. With much time on his hands for reading and reflecting, he began to recognize different movements and feelings arising within him. These came primarily from two different sources: the first were holy desires that arose from his reading about the life of Christ and the lives of various saints; the second were the vain and worldly hopes and desires that flowed from his daydreaming about the deeds of gallantry he would later perform in the service of a certain lady at court. Both of these alternating thoughts brought delight to him while he was reflecting on them, but gradually he came to notice a crucial difference between them. The delight and consolation from the worldly hopes and desires did not last and he was later left dry and dissatisfied. The holy desires and resolutions, however, continued to leave him consoled and satisfied even after he dismissed them from his mind. One day his eyes began to open, as he tells us, and he "came to recognize the difference between the two spirits that moved him, the one being from the evil spirit, the other from God."[4]

The extended period of prayer and penance at Manresa that followed his recovery at Loyola was a difficult but fruitful time for Ignatius. Although he was filled with much fervor and a great desire to advance in the service of God, he had, as he tells us, little knowledge of spiritual things. But gradually God led him to a greater understanding of his experiences, "just as a schoolmaster treats a little boy when he teaches him."[5] In learning his lessons one by one, he became more and more aware of the spirits that moved him and the source from which they came. This proved to be true in such cases as his tormenting anxieties with the sins of his past life, the time that should be allotted to needed sleep, the proper use of penitential practices, and the necessary care that should be taken of himself.

The mystical experience that took place by the river Cardoner at Manresa was of critical importance for this spiritual growth. Among other things, it illumined his understanding in such a way that he was able to apply a principle of discernment to *all* his experiences and to recognize the significance of his desires and consolations as well as their use and purpose in the spiritual life. In addition to the strong desire to serve God generously and the determination to persevere in his resolutions that were present from the time of his conversion at Loyola, there was now added a principle of *spiritual direction*. He came to see that the diverse and conflicting motions in his soul could come from different sources. They could be signs from God revealing his will; they could come from the evil one trying to seduce him away from God's will; or they could be due to his own prejudices. This growing capacity to recognize, separate, and identify these interior movements was something he would greatly value throughout his life.[6]

This process of discernment continued after Ignatius left Manresa and moved on again in his pilgrim journey. For example, we see it operative in his decision to remain in Jerusalem, and then changing it when he could not obtain the permission of the Franciscan provincial. We see this discerning process also taking place in his decision to embrace the life of a student in order to prepare him to help others and his recognition of which actions would help and which actions would hinder him during the years of schooling. During this long period of study he was also constantly seeking to aid others in the process of seeking and following God's will by sharing his own experiences and insights.

The process of group discernment was of great importance when Ignatius and the nine others who formed the early band of companions deliberated about their future together as a religious community. Their prayerful deliberations and discernment that took place at Rome in 1539 led to the decisions to form a new religious order in the church, to seek ecclesiastical approval for their way of life, and to elect Ignatius as the general superior.[7] Then, during his years as general superior, the process of discernment was an ongoing process in his work of leadership and governance. This was especially true in two areas: the painstaking and extended labors of drawing up the *Constitutions* for the new religious order, and the vast correspondence that was such an important aspect of these later years, especially his letters of spiritual direction where he sought to assist others to find and embrace God's will in their lives.

2. Discernment in the *Spiritual Exercises*

It is in the *Spiritual Exercises* that we find the most complete treatment of discernment by Ignatius. This is not the place to give a detailed account of that teaching but some main aspects of it should be summarized briefly.[8] Our treatment focuses first on his rules for discernment and then on his teaching that is concerned with the times and method of making a sound and good election (decision).

Ignatius gives us two sets of rules for the discernment of spirits in the *Spiritual Exercises*. The first set (##313–27) is more suitable for the First Week while the second set (##328–36) is more appropriate for the Second Week.[9] As noted earlier, the teaching in these rules flowed from Ignatius's experiences in his own prayer. He expects that those engaged in prayer during the course of the exercises will be moved and affected by different spirits just as he was. Some will come from a good source and will move a person toward God, while others will move in the opposite direction. Ignatius wants to bring a person to greater insights about these movements by identifying them and separating them as to their sources. It is a process of discerning and distinguishing the good spirits from the bad and then acting accordingly.

Rules for the First Week

The rules for the First Week begin with a clear contrast between the general procedure of the good spirit and that of the evil spirit. For persons who are alienated from God through sin and going from one serious sin to another, the enemy seeks to keep them complacent and at peace. However, for those who are seeking to overcome sin and make progress in the service of God, it is characteristic of the evil spirit to cause anxiety and discouragement. The way of the good spirit, however, is far different. For those complacent in a sinful way of life, the good spirit seeks to arouse them and sting their consciences with remorse. On the other hand, for those making progress, it is characteristic of the good spirit to encourage them and stir up holy desires so that a person may move forward in the service of God with confidence.

The rules go on to treat the interior motions of consolation and desolation, concepts that are extremely important for Ignatius. Spiritual consolation for him "includes every increase in hope, faith, and charity, and every interior joy which calls and attracts one toward heavenly things and to the salvation of one's soul, by bringing it tranquility and peace in its Creator and Lord" (#316). Thus, it is of the nature of consolation to lead and bring a person to God. Spiritual desolation, on the other hand, is the contrary to consolation. It leaves a person unhappy and feeling separated from God and it moves one away from a spirit of faith, hope, and love (#317).

Ignatius then gives some practical suggestions to those who find themselves in a state of consolation or desolation. Since it is the good spirit who is chiefly the one who guides us in times of consolation and the evil spirit who does this in times of desolation, a person should never make a change in a time of desolation. Rather, a person should remain patient and constant in one's prayer, trusting in God's ongoing grace and confident that the time of consolation will return. A state of desolation can keep us humble and aware of our total dependence on the abundant grace of God. On the other hand, during times of consolation we should not be puffed up with ourselves but ever mindful of our weakness during times of desolation and our need to store up strength for these future times.

The rules for the First Week conclude with some insights about the tactics of the enemy of our human nature. For example, he acts like a false lover who wants to remain secret and undetected in his evil intents. His evil intentions can be thwarted when a person is open with a confessor or some other spiritual person who understands his deceits. Ignatius also compares him to a military commander who carefully studies the strength of a particular fortification and then attacks it at its weakest point. In like manner the evil spirit attacks spiritual persons, not where they are strong and well defended, but where they are weakest and most vulnerable.

Rules for the Second Week

Since the rules that are more suitable for the Second Week are more subtle and probing in their treatment of spiritual consolation, we can only comment here on a few points. Ignatius in his own spiritual journey had slowly come to the realization that the state of consolation could be traced either to the action of God or to that of the evil spirit. This left him with the conviction that the best protection against the subtle deceptions of the evil one was an accurate knowledge of the nature and causes of consolation. This is what he wanted to make clear in his careful development of rules pertaining to the Second Week.

Ignatius distinguishes two types of consolation: consolation without a previous cause, and consolation by means of a previous cause. The former, consolation without a previous cause, arises apart from any perceived or recognized object. For Ignatius, only God can give this type of consolation to a person, for it is his prerogative alone to enter the soul, depart from it, and cause a motion "which draws the whole person into love of His Divine Majesty" (#330). Ignatius's remarks on this type of consolation are brief and later commentators of the *Exercises* have sought to fathom the exact meaning of this concept.[10]

He has much more to say about the second type, consolation by means of a preceding cause. When a cause precedes the consolation— that is, when the consolation comes from some object presented to the senses, the imagination, or the intellect—then either the good angel or the evil spirit may have helped to bring it about. The good angel consoles for the good of the soul, while the evil spirit "consoles" so that afterward he may draw the person to his own evil designs. Thus, the evil spirit assumes the *appearance* of an angel of light; he begins by suggesting suitable thoughts for devotion, and ends up by insinuating his own. A person, then, must be attentive to the whole course of his or her thoughts during consolation. If the beginning, middle, and end of the course of thoughts are good, it is a sign that they are from the good angel. If the train of thoughts terminates in something evil, distracting, or less good, or if they weaken the soul by destroying its peace and tranquility, then we have clear signs that the thoughts are proceeding from the evil spirit.

Saint Ignatius brings this series of rules for discernment to an end by returning to the consolation that comes about without any preceding cause. As mentioned earlier, this type of consolation can *only* come from God. Yet, one must carefully distinguish the actual time of the consolation and the period that follows it. During this period that follows, a person is still fervent and favored with the grace and aftereffects of the consolation that has passed. As a result, one might form various resolutions and plans "which are not granted directly by God our Lord" (#336). Therefore, these resolutions and decisions must be carefully examined before they are put into execution. This rule brings to mind Saint Ignatius's decision to remain permanently in the Holy Land, a decision that seems to have been made in the wake of great consolation, but one that was not confirmed or approved later by the ecclesiastical authority in the Holy Land.[11]

Discernment also plays a part in the instructions Ignatius gives on the three ways or times for making an election (decision). This is particularly true for the second way. In these instructions for making the election at the end of the Second Week, Saint Ignatius speaks of the three times when a correct and good choice of a way of life may be made. The first time or mode, rare in practice, is "when God so moves and attracts the will that a devout soul without hesitation, or the possibility of hesitation, follows what has been manifested to it" (#175). As examples of this, Ignatius points out that this is what Saint Paul and Saint Matthew did when Christ called them to follow him. The second time is "when much light and understanding are derived through experiences of desolations and consolations and discernment of the diverse spirits" (#176). This way, in other words, involves a person in the process of reflecting on the various interior movements that occurred during prayer and applying the rules for the discernment of spirits as a means to discover and embrace God's will. The third way occurs in a time of tranquility when a person is not moved by the interior movements of the soul that marked the second way. Here the decision is made by a calm analysis of and reflection on the various factors and the weighing of the pros and cons. In actual practice, the second and third ways often supplement one another. This is the way Ignatius himself often proceeded, as is clear from the accounts of his own decision making in the pages of his *Spiritual Diary*.

3. Discernment in Daily Life

It should be stressed at this point that Ignatius never intended that the knowledge of the discernment of spirits should remain on the objective and theoretical level. His teaching on this subject was to be directed to *practical application*. His rules and instructions were meant as helps and guides for the person who was actually experiencing the various movements of the spirit. This is clear from the role the discernment of spirits played in his own life and the role he expected this process to unfold in the experience of those making the spiritual exercises. It is abundantly clear from the text of the *Exercises*, especially the "Introductory Annotations," that Ignatius expected the retreatant to undergo and experience various movements. He certainly does *not* expect the retreatant to be led blindly by these movements. On the contrary, he wants the retreatant to reflect on them, to identify them, to recognize them as good or bad, and through them to purify himself or herself of inordinate affections, and to seek God's will generously and purely.

But it should also be stressed that Ignatius expected this process of discernment to continue outside of the time a person is engaged specifically in making the exercises. He expected discernment to be an ongoing process in the lives of those who were seeking to find God in their daily lives.

After his own serious turning to God that followed his conversion at Loyola castle, Ignatius continually sought to assist others to find God's will in their lives and to follow it generously. He did this, of course, while directing others in the spiritual exercises, but he also sought to do this through his numerous letters of spiritual direction. These letters were directed to people in all walks of life. A good example of this is the often quoted letter to a religious woman who sought his spiritual guidance, Sister Teresa Rejadell. He writes to her in one letter:

> The enemy is leading you into error in two things, but not in any way to make you fall into a sin that would separate you from God our Lord. He tries rather to upset you and to interfere with your service of God and your peace of mind. In the first place he proposes and leads you on to a false humility. And in the second, he gives you an exaggerated fear of God, with which you are altogether too much occupied.[12]

Ignatius goes on in the course of the letter to develop these points more fully in order to assist her to recognize God's authentic movement in her daily life.

The importance Ignatius gives to the general examen of conscience has already been noted in the chapter on prayer. But its importance in Ignatius's mind should be recalled once again in the context of discernment in daily life. Ignatius always valued this method of prayer as a graced opportunity for a person to be mindful each day of God's action in one's life. It is a daily method of prayer that enables a person to be more sensitive to the many ways God works in one's life and thus grow in the capacity to find God in all the circumstances of one's life. It is an examen of consciousness because it helps a person to become more conscious of the workings of God in one's unique life. It gives a person the daily opportunity to ask oneself: "Where have I found God in my life today? Where have I experienced his presence in the ordinary circumstances of my life?" It enables a person to notice things in a more careful manner and thus grow in the capacity to find God in all things. It helps to integrate one's prayer and daily life and it furthers the movement toward becoming a more effective contemplative in action for the greater glory of God.[13]

Conclusion

This chapter has presented only a few aspects of discernment in the Ignatian tradition. Before concluding, however, it is good to recall some basic points that are central to the whole process of discernment. First, it is important to stress that the basis of any discernment has to be the deep and ongoing prayer of the persons involved in the process. The context of *any* true discernment is prayer. When decisions need to be made in the discerning process, it is important that they be made in the context of faith and prayer. Unless there is a corresponding desire to seek and find God continually in our lives and to deepen our awareness of his reality and presence, discernment will not be effective.

In addition to a deep and constant spirit of prayer, discernment also calls for an attitude of freedom and detachment. This is an attitude that allows a person to give God and his will the central place in one's life. It is a freedom and detachment from all other things that would either prevent or hinder one's striving to focus on God. It is the sense of freedom that allows God to become and remain the central reality in one's life. It is a stance before God that is summed up in the words of the psalmist, "Here I am; in the scroll of the book it is written of me. I delight to do your will, O my God" (Ps 40:7–8).

Although discernment in general is an inward-looking process, there should always be an outward thrust connected to it. A deepening union with God should lead to a deepening union with others. An increasing sense of compassion for others and their needs should flow from one's union with God. Finally, the process should lead to an increasing sensitivity to life and all its mysteries, to an increasing awareness of God's presence in all things, and to our growth as contemplatives in action.[14]

6

THE CONSTITUTIONS

It has often been noted that the *Constitutions of the Society of Jesus* are as important as the *Spiritual Exercises* for understanding the spiritual teaching of Saint Ignatius.[1] Behind all the norms and directives contained in this document lies that same spirit of apostolic service carried out for the greater glory of God that marked Ignatius's own spiritual quest and the spiritual vision of the *Spiritual Exercises*. The many years that Ignatius gave to the careful composition of the *Constitutions* clearly attest to the great importance and significance he attached to this document. He wanted this written legacy to articulate in an organized and coherent form the basic thrust of his vision and also be a source of inspiration for the order he had founded. He intended it to be a dynamic source for the way of living, the "way of proceeding," that would characterize the spiritual and apostolic lives of those who wanted to follow in his footsteps as companions of Jesus.

1. The Process of Composition

When Saint Ignatius and the nine other founding fathers made the crucial decision in 1539 to form a new religious order, they drew up a brief document that described the basic purpose and spirit of the group and the apostolic vision in the service of

God that would be distinctive of the members. This document, now known as the *Formula of the Institute*, was submitted to Pope Paul III and incorporated into the papal bull that formally approved the new order in 1540. The *Formula of the Institute* can thus be considered the fundamental "Rule for the Society of Jesus," although it authorized its members to develop and expand this foundational document with more specific *Constitutions*.

When Saint Ignatius was elected superior general in 1541, he began the task of fulfilling this commission. He clearly saw the importance of this undertaking for the future welfare of the new order, and he gave himself to the laborious work of composition in a careful and painstaking manner. He brought many gifts to the writing of the *Constitutions*. He was a born leader of others and he was keenly alert to the needs of the times. Above all, he brought a spirit of prayer and a love of God that permeated all the practical decisions he had to make in the course of the writing. The glory, praise, and service of God were always foremost in his mind. When he was faced with making a decision, great or small, the guiding principle was always to choose the option that would bring greater glory to God.[2] In his prayer he constantly begged for the light to decide which choice would ultimately lead to this.

As we have seen, Ignatius was a mystic and a person gifted with a prayer of infused contemplation. But is important to note that he wedded these gifts of mystical prayer with the process of making concrete and practical decisions. This emerges clearly in the pages of the *Spiritual Diary* that were written by Ignatius while he was composing the *Constitutions*, particularly when he was trying to make decisions about the kind of poverty the *Constitutions* would prescribe. They lead us to conclude "that to a large extent these *Constitutions* are the fruit of his mystical contemplation and his natural prudence, united in a harmonious balance."[3]

Saint Ignatius was a clear thinker and organizer but not a particularly gifted writer, and so the actual writing of the *Con-*

stitutions initially proceeded somewhat slowly and at an irregular pace. This changed dramatically when Ignatius appointed Juan Polanco as his secretary in March 1547 and asked him to work with him on the writing of the *Constitutions*. Polanco was eminently qualified for this role, for he brought many literary and organizational skills to the work of composition.

The writing of the *Constitutions* progressed steadily so that by 1550 the first complete Spanish text was completed. Ignatius then summoned a representative number of professed fathers to Rome to discuss the text. They met in Rome in the early part of 1551 and, after discussing the document and making suggestions, they approved the work as a whole. Ignatius, however, regarded this as only a step in the process of approval. He wanted the final decision to be left to the General Congregation that would meet after his death to elect his successor. In the meantime, he clearly saw the value of having a period in which the *Constitutions* could be promulgated and made known on an experimental basis that would provide further consultation.

Jerónimo Nadal's assistance in this process was invaluable. Ignatius appointed him to travel extensively to Jesuit houses to explain the *Constitutions* and promulgate them for experimental use. During 1552–55 he first visited the Jesuit communities in Sicily, Spain, and Portugal, and then the houses in Germany, Austria, and Italy. By means of these travels, he was able to make the *Constitutions* widely known in a personal way and was also able to send back helpful reports to Ignatius, who continued to make revisions right up to the time of his death. The *Constitutions* finally became authoritative for the Society of Jesus when the First General Congregation approved Ignatius's Autograph Spanish Text and the Latin translation made by Polanco in 1558.[4]

2. Structure of the *Constitutions*

The main text of the *Constitutions* is drawn up in ten parts, preceded by two preliminary documents: the *Formula of the Institute* and the *General Examen*. The *Examen* and the *Constitutions* are both augmented by *Declarations* that serve as authoritative explanations and clarifications of the respective texts. The *Formula*, as we have seen, is the brief document written by Ignatius and the founding fathers that is inserted in the papal bulls of approval and forms the foundation for the *Constitutions*. The *General Examen* seeks to give to those who are thinking of entering the Society an overall description and understanding of the institute and the way of life of its members. It provides the opportunity for candidates to ponder this material during the probationary days that precede entrance into the novitiate.

Ignatius considered two ways of organizing the material for the ten parts of the *Constitutions*. The first would initially treat the whole body and its end, and then consider the means to attain the end. The second would focus initially on the individual members and then build to a treatment of the end, namely, the preservation and development of the entire body of the Society and its well-being. He opted for the second, the "order of execution," as he called it. Thus, the first seven parts treat the admission, formation, and definitive incorporation into the Society of its individual members, followed by the missioning of these members for various apostolic endeavors. Part VIII considers the relations and means of unity among the members themselves and with the superior general. Part IX focuses on the desired qualities and role of the superior general, while Part X concludes with a treatment of the body of the Society as a whole and its preservation, development, and well-being. Ignatius ends his introduction with the words: "This is the order which will be followed in the *Constitutions* and *Declarations* while we keep our attention fixed on the end which all of us are seeking, the glory and praise of God our Creator and Lord."⁵

3. Key Aspects of the *Constitutions*

This chapter certainly cannot give any kind of a full treatment of the content of the *Constitutions*. It simply provides a summary of some of the main points that emerge prominently in its pages. The focus is on those parts that bring out the main thrust of Ignatius's spiritual vision as well as the spiritual motivation, ideals, and principles that are fundamental to the legislative prescriptions. The close connection between Ignatius's teaching in the *Constitutions* and the *Spiritual Exercises* should constantly be kept in mind. Before proceeding to the main parts of the *Constitutions* themselves, we briefly treat the two preliminary documents, the *Formula of the Institute* and the *General Examen*.

a. THE *FORMULA OF THE INSTITUTE*

It should be recalled once again that there are *two* versions of the *Formula of the Institute*. The first was drawn up by Ignatius and the other founding fathers and included in the initial papal apostolic letter of approval by Pope Paul III in 1540. This relatively brief document was slightly revised and augmented later and incorporated in the second papal document of approval, *Exposcit debitum*, promulgated by Pope Julius III in 1550. These two versions are often printed side by side in texts of the *Constitutions*.⁶

As the foundational document, the *Formula of the Institute* presents in seed form the key points that will be developed more fully in the ten parts of the *Constitutions*. These include the strong apostolic thrust of the order, with the members striving for the spread of the faith and the progress of souls in Christian life and doctrine through various ministries; a special vow of obedience to the Holy Father for missions of any kind; a willing obedience to the superior general elected from the members; a lifestyle marked by evangelical poverty; the novel private recitation of the Divine Office rather than the traditional chant in common in order to be more available for the apostolic ministries; and a final profession in the Society only after a long period of testing.

b. THE *GENERAL EXAMEN* AND ITS DECLARATIONS

The *General Examen* is intended for those who wish to enter the Society. It seeks to provide them with a summary of the institute and the way of life of its members. It can assist an examiner to determine a candidate's suitability for this particular way of religious life, as well as provide the opportunity for the candidate to ponder the material during the early days of probation. At the beginning it states the overall end: "The end of this Society is to devote itself with God's grace not only to the salvation and perfection of the members' own souls, but also with that same grace to labor strenuously in giving aid toward the salvation and perfection of the souls of their neighbors" (# 3). In order to achieve this end more effectively, the members will take vows of obedience, poverty, and chastity. In addition to these traditional religious vows, the professed fathers will also pronounce a fourth vow of special obedience to the Holy Father regarding apostolic missions.

Much of the eight chapters of the *General Examen* involves questions seeking to clarify the candidate's suitability for this way of life and to see if there are any canonical impediments that would bar admission. Chapter 4, however, is particularly important for Ignatian spirituality. For example, there is a passage that emphasizes that spirit of abnegation that was so dear to the heart of Saint Ignatius. He obviously wanted the candidate to be aware, even at this early stage, that a demanding spirit of humility and abnegation for the love of Christ should mark the religious and apostolic life of a Jesuit. In words very similar to the spirit of the meditations on the *Three Kinds of Humility* and the *Three Classes of Men* from the Second Week of the *Spiritual Exercises*, Ignatius writes:

> It is likewise very important to bring to the attention of those who are being examined, emphasizing it and giving it great weight in the sight of our Creator and Lord, to how great a degree it helps and profits in the spiritual life to abhor in its totality and not in part whatever the world loves and embraces, and to accept and desire with all possible energy whatever Christ our Lord has loved and embraced. Just as the men of the world who follow the world love and seek with such great diligence honors, fame, and esteem for a great name on earth, as the world teaches them, so those who proceed spiritually and truly follow Christ our Lord love and intensely desire everything opposite. (#101)

After spelling out these desires in further concrete detail, Ignatius adds that the candidate should be asked whether he finds in himself such desires. He recognizes, however, that not all candidates will be able to answer affirmatively at the time since it does call for a high degree of generosity and commitment. Still, he would want the candidate to at least have a *desire* to experience them, for Ignatius was convinced that "the better to arrive at this degree of perfection which is so precious in the spiritual life, his chief and most earnest endeavor should be to seek in our Lord his greater abnegation and continual mortification in all things possible" (#103).

---

c. The *Constitutions* and Their Declarations

Two points should be emphasized before we look at some key aspects in the ten parts of the *Constitutions*. First, the end of the Society and its apostolic thrust are never lost from view. This is constantly kept in mind throughout these pages with such recurring phrases as "God's greater glory" and "the service of God." This is the supreme norm that should guide and direct everything else. Second, there is the priority given to God's grace. Ignatius knows that human means and endeavors have to be employed and that there has to be some form of written constitutions drawn up by human hands. But ultimately it is to God's assistance that one must look for the guidance, protection, and growth of the Society. Ignatius brings this out clearly in the preamble to the *Constitutions*, where he emphasizes that "God our Creator and Lord is the one who in his Supreme Wisdom and Goodness must preserve, direct, and carry forward in his divine service this least Society of Jesus, just as he deigned to begin it." What helps most toward this end is "the interior law of charity and love which the Holy Spirit writes and imprints upon hearts" (#134).

The first chapter of Part III treats the spiritual training of novices, those who have been admitted and are in the early stages of probation. It focuses on the various means that should be employed to preserve their vocation and assist them "to make progress, both in spirit and in virtues, along the path of the divine service" (#243). Ignatius gives careful advice with attention to details and we find him writing: "All should take special care to guard with great diligence the gates of their senses (especially the eyes, ears, and tongue) from all disorder, to preserve themselves in peace and true humility of their souls, and to show this by their silence when it should be kept and, when they must speak, by the discretion and edification of their words, the modesty of their countenance, the maturity of their walk, and all their movements, without giving any sign of impatience or pride" (#250). He also adds:

> They should be taught how to guard themselves from the illusions of the devil in their devotions and how to defend themselves from all temptations. They should know the means which may exist for overcoming these and applying themselves to the pursuit of the true and solid virtues, whether with many spiritual visitations or with fewer, by endeavoring always to go forward in the path of the divine service. (#260)

Time should be given to spiritual things and all should strive to acquire as much devotion as given by God's grace. All should make diligent efforts to keep their intention right, always aiming to serve and please the Divine Goodness, and they should often be exhorted to seek God Our Lord in all things (#288).

The importance of living the vows of religious life is also highlighted. For example, "all should love poverty as a mother, and according to the measure of holy discretion all should, when occasions arise, feel some of its effects" (#287). Likewise, "it is very helpful for making progress and highly necessary that all devote themselves to complete obedience, recognizing the superior, whoever he is, as being in the place of Christ Our Lord and maintaining interior reverence and love for him" (#284).

The somewhat lengthy fourth part of the *Constitutions* is given over to the education of those who have completed the novitiate training (the approved scholastics). Again, Ignatius situates the pursuit of a solid foundation in learning within the context of the apostolic end of the Society of Jesus. A systematic program of learning is necessary for those who are seeking to devote themselves to various apostolic ministries throughout the world in the service of God, Creator and Lord. In this section of the *Constitutions* Ignatius lays down careful instructions about the programs of education and instruction that are to be carried out in the colleges and universities of the Society. In doing so, he gives clear evidence that he deserves a place among history's significant educators.

Ignatius wanted the approved scholastics to continue their spiritual growth and not grow tepid in their love of true virtues and the religious life; but he also did not want their studies to be hindered by practices of penance and long prayers and meditations. He was convinced that God could be found in the process of study and that "their devoting themselves to learning, which they acquire with a pure intention of serving God and which in a certain way requires the whole person, will be not less but rather more pleasing to God our Lord during the time of study" (#340). On a practical note, he stipulates that in addition to regular confession and communion and daily Mass, they will devote an hour each day to prayer. During this hour, they will recite the Hours of Our Lady (The Little Office), examine their conscience twice each day, and add other prayers according to one's devotion.

Part VI of the *Constitutions* focuses on the personal life of those already admitted and incorporated into the body of the Society as professed fathers or formed coadjutors (Part V had treated the requirements and procedures for this incorporation). The apostolic thrust of the Society remains foremost in Ignatius's mind, and so he seeks here to emphasize the means that can assist the members to apply themselves more generously and fruitfully to the service of God and the aid of others in their varied ministries.

The observance of the religious vows of poverty, chastity, and obedience remains central and so Ignatius develops further reflections on the vows, particularly obedience and poverty. For example, he urges:

> All should strongly dispose themselves to observe obedience and to distinguish themselves in it.... They should

keep in view God our Creator and Lord, for whom such
obedience is practiced, and endeavor to proceed in a spirit
of love and not as men troubled by fear....Consequently,
in all things into which obedience can with charity be
extended, we should be ready to receive its command just
as if it were coming from Christ our Savior, since we are
practicing the obedience to one in his place and because of
love and reverence for him. (#547)

No less emphasis is placed on poverty: "Poverty, as the strong
wall of the religious institute, should be loved and preserved in its
integrity as far as this is possible with God's grace" (#553). Ignatius
is particularly concerned that this defense of the religious life
should not be weakened since he realistically knows from the witness of history that a fervent observance of poverty can gradually
decline over a period of time. He writes:

The enemy of the human race generally tries to weaken
this defense and rampart which God our Lord inspired
religious Institutes to raise against him and the other
adversaries of their perfection. Into what was well
ordered by their first founders he induces alterations by
means of interpretations and innovations not in conformity with those founders' first spirit. (#553)

Regarding the spiritual life and religious practices of the
formed and experienced Jesuits, Ignatius presupposes that they will
"run in the way of Christ our Lord" to the extent they can.
Furthermore, he wants to seek a balance between doing too much
on one hand and doing too little on the other. It should be a discerning love that guides the individual in consultation with his confessor or superior. Thus Ignatius writes:

In what pertains to prayer, meditation, and study, and also in regard to the bodily practices of fasts, vigils, and other austerities of penances, it does not seem proper to give them any other rule than that which discreet charity dictates to them....On the one hand, they should take care that the excessive use of these practices not weaken their bodily strength and or [*sic*] take up so much time that they are rendered incapable of helping the neighbor spiritually according to our Institute; on the other hand, they should be vigilant that these practices not be relaxed to such an extent that the spirit grows cold and the human and lower passions grow warm. (#582)[7]

Part VII of the *Constitutions* returns to the apostolic missions undertaken by the formed members of the Society and their various ministries among God's people. The idea of the Jesuit being missioned for this apostolic work is central to Ignatius's vision. In keeping with the spirit of the fourth vow of the professed fathers to the pope, Ignatius focuses first on missions entrusted to the Society by the Holy Father, and then the various missions commissioned by the superiors of the Society. While treating of the various norms and criteria for choosing ministries, Ignatius once again highlights his simple and fundamental criterion, namely, "having the greater service of God and the more universal good before one's eyes as the guiding norm" (#622).

Ignatius realized that the various apostolic missions would disperse the members of the Society and bring them to many different parts of the world. This led him in Part VIII of the *Constitutions* to consider the various helps that would foster unity with the superior general and among themselves. He knew that this unity was essential for the preservation of the Society and the attaining of its end. Thus, in this section he treats such various topics as the role of obedience, the important function of superiors, the value of the exchange of letters, and the occasions for holding a General Congregation. But above all it would be the mutual love of God that would do the most to maintain this desired unity of hearts and minds. Ignatius writes:

> On both sides, the chief bond to cement the union of the members among themselves and with their head is the love of God our Lord. For when the superior and the subjects are closely united to his Divine and Supreme Goodness, they will very easily be united among themselves, through that same love which will descend from the Divine Goodness and spread to all other persons, and particularly to the body of the Society. (#671)

Part IX of the *Constitutions* focuses on the superior general, elected for life to be the head of the Society. In Ignatius's mind, the role of the superior general is crucial, for he holds the charge of the entire body and has the responsibility for the good government, preservation, and development of the whole body.

In chapter 2 of Part IX, Ignatius presents a description of the kind of person the superior general should be and the qualities that are desirable in him This well-known passage can be looked upon as a "spirituality for superiors" as well as one that provides all Jesuits with an ideal they can seek to approach.[8] Six qualities are enumerated and their overall importance is indicated by the order in which they are listed.[9] Above all, the superior general should be a man of God and prayer. "He should be closely united with God our Lord and have familiarity with him in prayer and in all his operations" (#723). Second, he should be a person whose example in virtue should be a help to other members of the Society. His life should be marked particularly by an ardent charity for others, a genuine humility that will make him "highly beloved of God our Lord and of human beings," and one that is free from all inordinate affections. A spirit of magnanimity and fortitude of soul is also extremely important, for he will have to initiate great undertakings in the service of God and persevere steadfastly in the face of various challenges. Third, he should be endowed with great intelligence and judgment, a man of discernment who can deal with both speculative and practical matters as they arise. Fourth, he should be "vigilant and solicitous in undertaking enterprises and vigorous in carrying them through to their completion and perfection" (#730). Fifth, he should have the health, appearance, appropriate age, and physical energy that will enable him to fulfill his office to the glory of God. The sixth quality lists some external things that can be a means for further edification and the service of God, such as esteem, a good reputation, "and whatever else contributes toward authority among those within and without" (#733).

The tenth and final part of the *Constitutions* serves as a conclusion and sums up many of the points that were developed earlier. Saint Ignatius here seeks to summarize those aspects that are essential for the preservation and development of the whole body of the Society. He values *both* the supernatural means *and* the natural, but he clearly gives priority to the former. As he writes at the beginning of Part X in a manner so similar to the way he introduced the *Constitutions*: "The Society was not instituted by human means; and it is not through them that it can be preserved and increased, but through the omnipotent hand of Christ, our God and Lord. Therefore in him alone must be placed the hope that he will preserve and carry forward what he deigned to begin for his service and praise and for the aid of souls" (#812). Thus, the members of the Society should constantly offer prayers and Masses for this holy intention.

Developing this point further, Ignatius stresses the importance of the members of the Society being closely united instruments in the hands of God. The means that foster this unity are highlighted: goodness and virtue, especially charity; a pure intention for divine service; familiarity with God through spiritual exercises of devotion; and sincere zeal for souls for the greater glory of God. Ignatius concludes: "Thus, it appears that care should be taken in general that all the members of the Society devote themselves to the solid and perfect virtues and to spiritual pursuits, and attach greater importance to them than to learning and other natural and human gifts" (#813). Only in this way can one's apostolic endeavors bear fruit and be efficacious.

Ignatius also recognized and valued the natural gifts and means that can enable his followers to be effective workers in the Lord's vineyard. Grace does build on nature. And so he writes:

> God desires to be glorified both through the natural means, which he gives as Creator, and through the supernatural means which he gives as the Author of grace. Therefore the human or acquired means ought to be sought with diligence, especially well grounded and solid learning, and a method of proposing it to the people by means of sermons, lectures, and the art of dealing and conversing with others. (#814)

A few other key points can be mentioned here. Ignatius again reiterates the importance of poverty for the preservation and development of the Society, since it is the "bulwark of religious institutes" and the primary means of avoiding any spirit of avarice. All forms of ambition must also be precluded for the overall good of the Society, and so its members must never seek, directly or indirectly, any dignity, honor, or prelacy within or outside the Society. Finally, the union of minds and hearts among the members is again brought to the fore as Ignatius writes simply and directly: "Whatever helps toward the union of the members of this Society among themselves and with their head will also help much toward preserving the well being of the Society" (#821).

d. Revision of the Society Law and the Complementary Norms

In its decree on the renewal of religious life (*Perfectae caritatis*, no. 2), the Second Vatican Council spoke of two necessary measures for an appropriate renewal of religious communities: first, an ongoing return to the sources of all Christian life and to the original spirit and inspiration of a community's unique beginnings; second, an application and adjustment of that spirit and inspiration to the changed conditions of the times. The Thirty-First General Congregation (1964–65) and the Thirty-Second General Congregation (1974–75) began and implemented this process for the Society of Jesus, seeking to adapt the Society's way of life and apostolate to the needs of the times, while at the same time preserving a fidelity to its unique charism and original mission.

At a later time, the Thirty-Third General Congregation (1983) mandated that a complete revision be made of the legislation particular to the Society of Jesus after the promulgation of the new *Code of Canon Law for the Latin Church* (1983) and the *Code of Canon Law of the Eastern Churches* (1993). This task, after much study and preparation, was brought to a successful conclusion by the Thirty-Fourth General Congregation that met in 1995.

Certain guidelines were carefully followed in this undertaking. First, the *Constitutions* of Saint Ignatius were to maintain a central and very real place in Jesuit law and continue to inspire and govern all aspects of Jesuit life. In order to facilitate this, notes of clarification, modification, and updating (approved by a General Congregation) were to be appended to the original Ignatian text without making any changes in the latter. Second, pertinent decrees and statements of subsequent General Congregations that express the spirit of the *Constitutions* and are important and helpful for the ongoing renewal of Jesuit life and apostolate were to be reformulated and arranged according to the order of the *Constitutions* themselves. They were to have a "permanent relationship to those *Constitutions* as their 'Complementary Norms,' approved by a general congregation and alterable only by such a congregation."[10] Finally, in future publications, the *Constitutions* and the *Complementary Norms* were to be published in one and the same volume, "so that the living internal unity that exists between these two parts of our law might shine forth more clearly and their ongoing spiritual identity might be more obvious."[11]

Conclusion

This brief description of the relationship between the original Ignatian *Constitutions* and the more recent *Complementary Norms* once again highlights the healthy tension that must be maintained between the old and the new, the traditional and the contemporary. In fulfilling its present-day mission, the Society of Jesus seeks to be as attentive and responsive to the particular needs of the times (as Saint Ignatius was in his lifetime), while also being faithful to the spiritual heritage it received from its founder. Some of the main issues and challenges of the contemporary scene are presented in the following chapter.

7

CONTEMPORARY ISSUES AND CHALLENGES

As mentioned previously, the Second Vatican Council (1962–65), in its call for the renewal of religious life, urged all religious orders and institutes to renew themselves by a twofold process: first, a return to the original charism and inspiration behind a given religious community; second, an appropriate adaptation of the community to the changed conditions of the times. The Society of Jesus responded to this challenge under the leadership of its superiors general (Reverend Father Pedro Arrupe, 1965–83, and Reverend Father Peter-Hans Kolvenbach, 1983–2008), and the four General Congregations of the Society that met at intervals over the course of those years, Thirty-First General Congregation (1964–65), Thirty-Second General Congregation (1974–75), Thirty-Third General Congregation (1983), and Thirty-Fourth General Congregation (1995). The most recent General Congregation (Thirty-Fifth [2008]) elected Reverend Father Adolfo Nicholás as the new superior general.

The call for a return to the sources brought forth an impressive number of writings, both scholarly and practical, on various aspects of Ignatian spirituality. There were studies on the *Spiritual Exercises*, the *Constitutions*, Ignatian prayer and discernment, and many other aspects of Jesuit religious life and mission. Much of what was published in English was spearheaded by the ongoing work of the Institute of Jesuit Sources in St. Louis, under the leadership of its founder, George Ganss, SJ, and his successor, John W. Padberg, SJ. In addition, many related studies have come forth in the series Studies in the Spirituality of Jesuits, published by the Seminar on Jesuit Spirituality.

This chapter highlights some of the major developments that have emerged in this process of renewal in Ignatian spirituality. They include the more inward aspects that look to Jesuit identity, way of life, sources of spiritual support, as well as the outward aspects that focus more on the Society's mission and choice of apostolic ministries. This is in keeping with the end of the Society, which is "to devote itself with God's grace not only to the salvation and perfection of the members' own souls, but also with that same grace to labor strenuously in giving aid toward the salvation and perfection of the souls of their neighbors" (*Constitutions*, # 3). Both of these aspects, of course, are intimately connected and should be integrated in the life of a Jesuit.

1. Renewal of the *Spiritual Exercises*

The renewal of the *Spiritual Exercises* coincided with the overall interest that developed in spirituality and prayer in the early 1970s, a movement that took many different forms. It was a time that especially witnessed a strong and continued interest in reviving and retrieving the classical spiritual writings of the Christian tradition. The return to the sources that took place in Ignatian spirituality was also clearly evident in such other influential schools of spirituality as the Benedictine, Franciscan, Dominican, Carmelite, and Norbetine. A renewed interest in various methods of prayer, particularly those of a contemplative bent, was also highly visible and the retreat movement took on a new and vibrant life.

In addition to the many excellent studies on various aspects of the *Spiritual Exercises* that were published, there took place a distinct and rather widespread movement in the actual practice of giving and making the spiritual exercises. This movement developed particularly in two major areas: first, the individually directed retreat; second, the making of the exercises while engaged in daily life, usually referred to as the "nineteenth annotation" retreat.

a. THE DIRECTED RETREAT

It will be recalled that Saint Ignatius throughout his life directed others in the spiritual exercises on a one-on-one basis, adapting them to the particular needs of an individual. This was the standard practice of his first companions as well as the early Jesuits who followed them. Over time, however, it became much more the norm to give the spiritual exercises to larger groups, even in the case of the full exercises of thirty days. Talks based on the *Exercises* were given to the retreatants at certain times during the day as a preparation and guidance for later prayer by the individual. This became the norm when Jesuits in formation made the thirty-day retreat in the novitiate or tertianship year or at the time of the annual eight-day retreat. This was also the case when retreats based on the *Exercises* were given to priests, religious, and laymen and laywomen. Although much good was accomplished in these large preached retreats, the focus tended to be on the conferences and talks of the director rather than on the prayer of the individual.

The late 1960s and the early 1970s witnessed a return to the early manner of making the exercises, and what came to be known as "an individually directed retreat" began to enjoy widespread popularity. The focus in this type of retreat is on the personal prayer of the individual, for a person devotes a significant part of each day to periods of prayer in an atmosphere of silence and attentiveness to God that could last from the more usual duration of eight days to the extended, long retreat of thirty days. Central to this way of making the exercises is the role of the director. The retreatants see the director once a day to talk over what is happening as they seek to open themselves to God in prayer and to become more sensitive to the promptings of the Holy Spirit deep in their own hearts, and also to receive suggestions for the following day's prayer. The primary director in the directed retreat is, of course, the Holy Spirit and this is something the director must always keep in mind. The director's main role is to assist and encourage the retreatants to become sensitive to the movements of the Spirit within them and to be attentive to God's gentle touch. This is in keeping with the introductory explanation (annotation) in the *Spiritual Exercises*, where Ignatius speaks of the Creator and Lord communicating himself to the devout soul. Here he writes that "the director should allow the Creator to deal immediately with the creature and the creature with its Creator and Lord" (#15).

Saint Ignatius always looked upon the spiritual exercises as a school for prayer, and so it should come as no surprise that the directed retreat movement brought with it a renewed interest in the various methods of prayer that are suggested in the pages of the *Exercises*. Many were particularly helped by a contemplative and scripturally based approach that did much to deepen their spirit of prayer.

This renewal of the *Spiritual Exercises* and Ignatian prayer also gave rise to a number of practical programs that focused on the training of retreat and spiritual directors in the Ignatian tradition. These programs were developed at such varied sites as retreat houses, spirituality centers, and academic settings. Participants came from all walks of life and included Jesuits, other religious men and women, and a significant number of laymen and laywomen. This did much to spread the influence of the *Spiritual Exercises* far and wide in both Catholic and ecumenical circles.

b. Nineteenth Annotation Retreat

Even Saint Ignatius himself realized that not everyone could set aside some thirty consecutive days to make the spiritual exercises in their entirety. Thus, in number 19 of his *Annotations* ("Introductory Explanations"), he speaks of a person who "is involved in public affairs or pressing occupations" taking an hour and a half of prayer each day and going through the exercises with a director over an extended period of time. This is the basis for the revived way of making the exercises that has come to be known as the nineteenth annotation retreat or the spiritual exercises made in everyday life.

As is the case with the directed retreat, this can also take different forms. The retreatant can meet with a director once a week over the course of several months to talk over his or her prayer during the preceding week and to receive pertinent material and suggestions for the following week. This would continue until one has gone through the full four weeks of the exercises. A person could also make the complete exercises as part of a small group that meets weekly with a leader (or leaders) of the group to share with one another what took place in prayer during the preceding week as well as receive material for prayer for the following week. Since these retreats take place while a person is engaged in one's normal duties and occupations, many have been helped to integrate their prayer with their daily concerns and occupations. It should be noted that as these types of retreat have grown in popularity, there has correspondingly emerged a great deal of helpful material for both directors and retreatants.[1]

This contemporary renewal of interest in making the spiritual exercises did much, then, to deepen and nourish the prayer lives of those seeking God. In fact, the making of the exercises as a means to achieve a deeper and more intimate union with God through contemplative prayer took on more and more importance.

This emphasis was present as well in the writings of various commentators on the *Exercises*.[2]

Finally, it is important to keep in mind that this revival of the spiritual exercises was *not* confined to the practice of giving and making them. There was also a renewed awareness of the importance of the exercises in the ongoing spiritual life of every Jesuit. This is brought out clearly in the documents of the Thirty-First General Congregation where it is stated: "To maintain faithfully the grace of our vocation as described in the Institute, the Spiritual Exercises of our holy founder stand in first place"[3] and "the Jesuit apostle goes from the Exercises, at once a school of prayer and of the apostolate, a man called by his vocation to be a contemplative in action."[4] The Thirty-Second Congregation, reiterating this emphasis, states:

> In the Spiritual Exercises we are able continually to renew our faith and apostolic hope by experiencing again the love of God in Christ Jesus. We strengthen our commitment to be companions of Jesus in His mission, to labor like Him in solidarity with the poor and with Him for the establishment of the Kingdom.[5]

Also emphasized by the same Congregation is the central ministry of the exercises:

> The ministry of the Spiritual Exercises is one of the most important we can undertake today. We should by all means encourage studies, research and experiment directed toward helping our contemporaries experience the vitality of the Exercises as adapted to the new needs which are theirs. Moreover the spirit of the Exercises should pervade every other ministry of the Word that we undertake.[6]

2. Discernment

This contemporary renewal of the *Spiritual Exercises* brought with it a widespread recognition of the importance and significance of the practice of discernment. A number of factors played a part in the awareness and appreciation that developed in this area. The many studies that were part of the return to the sources of Ignatian spirituality once again highlighted the central and essential role discernment played in Saint Ignatius's own life as well as in the pages of the *Spiritual Exercises*. There was also the strong desire of many to deepen their own personal relationship with God, find God in the daily events of their lives, and make any decisions in the context of faith and prayer.

The individually directed retreat movement was extremely important in this regard. These retreats helped many people become more and more sensitive to and aware of their own experience of God in prayer and the ways God moves in their lives and speaks to them in the depths of their hearts. Retreat directors, too, became more attentive to Saint Ignatius's injunction at the beginning of the *Exercises* "to allow the Creator to deal immediately with the creature and the creature with its Creator and Lord" (#15). There was also a greater appreciation of individuals' particular needs and a renewed awareness of the unique (and sometimes inscrutable) ways the Holy Spirit works in the lives of individuals.

The process of discernment focuses on the ongoing attempts to clarify and ascertain God's will in our lives and seeks to specify what actions and decisions are called for in the life of a person who wishes to follow Christ in a generous and total way. And since the process of discernment is intimately linked with a spirit of prayer, the context of any true discernment has to be one's ongoing prayer and the desire to be united with God. Discernment is fundamentally a process in prayer by which a person seeks attentively to recognize

God's will and respond faithfully and generously in the concrete circumstances of one's life.

As noted earlier, the Ignatian general examen is intimately connected with the process of discernment.[7] Thus, the awareness of the importance of discernment has brought with it a renewed appreciation of the examen as a means of becoming more aware of God's activity in our lives and more alert and sensitive to the many ways that a loving God moves and touches us. Ignatius highly regarded the examen as one of the principal means of seeking and finding God in all things in our daily lives.

3. The Apostolic Mission Today

The concept of *mission* is extremely important in Ignatian spirituality. It occupied a central place in Saint Ignatius's apostolic vision and it is spelled out in detail in the pages of the *Constitutions* and the subsequent decrees of the General Congregations of the Society. A Jesuit is fundamentally a person who has been "sent." As the Thirty-Second General Congregation states: "A Jesuit is essentially a man on mission: a mission which he receives immediately from the Holy Father and from his own religious superiors, but ultimately from Christ himself, the one sent by the Father. It is by being sent that the Jesuit becomes a companion of Jesus."[8]

The fundamental thrust of this missioning, this sending, must always be kept in mind. It is above all a sharing in Christ's mission, carried out as united companions of Jesus in the church under the leadership of the Roman pontiff, to whom the Society of Jesus has a special bond of love and service. It is a mission that must find its perennial source of renewal and effectiveness in the *Spiritual Exercises* and a mission that must be constantly nourished by a deep, personal love of God in Christ Jesus.

The mission, however, must be adapted to the particular needs and challenges of a given time. Just as Saint Ignatius contemplated his world in the sixteenth century, so, too, must the Society today contemplate its world and challenges. This has been a particular concern for the recent General Congregations. They have placed a high priority on discerning the "signs of the times" and articulating the best way that the Society can fulfill its mission in today's world.

The Thirty-First General Congregation (1965–66) in its two sessions sought to renew and update *all* aspects of Jesuit life in light of the significant directives of the Second Vatican Council. This congregation entitled its first decree *The Mission of the Society of Jesus Today* and stated at the beginning of this document that the Society was seeking "to take a very close look at its own nature and mission in order that, faithful to its own vocation, it can renew itself and adapt its life and its activities to the exigencies of the Church and the needs of contemporary man."[9] In the numerous decrees that followed, the members of this important congregation sought to fulfill this challenging task of renewal by looking at all aspects of Jesuit life. In the decree on the choice of ministries the traditional principles are reiterated: the greater service of God, universal good, the more pressing need, the great importance of a future good, and special care of those significant ministries for which Jesuits have special talent.[10]

The Thirty-Second General Congregation (1974–75) continued to put a strong emphasis on the renewal and adaptation of the Society to the contemporary needs of the church and the world. Decree 4 of this congregation, *Our Mission Today: The Service of Faith and the Promotion of Justice*, emphasized that the service of the faith was primary to the whole apostolate of the Society, while also stressing that the promotion of justice was an absolute requirement of such service. In the introduction to this decree, we read that "the mission of the Society of Jesus today is the service of faith, of which the promotion of justice is an absolute requirement. For reconciliation with God demands the reconciliation of people with one another."[11]

Decree 2 of this congregation, *Jesuits Today*, highlights this same point. In an often-quoted passage that describes Jesuit identity in our time we read:

> What is it to be a Jesuit? It is to know that one is a sinner, yet called to be a companion of Jesus as Ignatius was: Ignatius, who begged the Blessed Virgin to "place him with her Son," and who then saw the Father himself ask Jesus, carrying his Cross, to take this pilgrim into his company.
>
> What is it to be a companion of Jesus today? It is to engage, under the standard of the Cross, in the crucial struggle of our time: the struggle for faith and that struggle for justice which it includes.[12]

Again in the Thirty-Third General Congregation (1983), the question of apostolic mission held a central place in the deliberations. This is clearly indicated in its most important document, Decree 1, aptly entitled *Companions of Jesus Sent Into Today's World*. This title highlights the essential importance of the integration of the spiritual life and the apostolate, and we read at the beginning of this decree: "Only to the extent that he is united to God so that he be 'led gladly by the divine hand,' is a Jesuit 'a man on a mission.'"[13] This document confirmed the apostolic orientations set down by the previous two Congregations, particularly Decrees 2 and 4 of the Thirty-Second General Congregation, mentioned above. The conclusion of this decree aptly summarizes the mission of the Society in today's world:

In the task of announcing the Gospel, faith in Jesus Christ is first and last. It is a faith which comes alive only in works of love and justice. Our mission as Jesuits has, from the outset, been to seek the greater glory of God and the salvation of souls. Confirming "the service of faith of which the promotion of justice is an absolute requirement" as the contemporary expression of that mission, we look to the future and renew again our commitment in "a communion of life and work and sacrifice with the companions who have rallied round the same standard of the Cross and in fidelity to the Vicar of Christ, for the building up of a world at once more human and more divine."[14]

The Thirty-Fourth General Congregation (1995) regarded the orientation of the mission for today as one of its major works. While confirming the earlier thrusts of the previous Congregations, this gathering of Jesuits from around the world also emphasized some new dimensions, stressing "that our mission of the service of faith and the promotion of justice must be broadened to include, as integral dimensions, proclamation of the Gospel, dialogue, and the evangelization of culture."[15] Thus, Decree 4 focused on "Our Mission and Culture" and Decree 5 on "Our Mission and Interreligious Dialogue."

This Congregation particularly recognized the importance of collaboration with the laity, developing its key points in the decree on "Cooperation with the Laity in Mission." The conclusion to this document succinctly summarizes the main aspects of this collaboration:

Cooperation with the laity is both a constitutive element of our way of proceeding and a grace calling for individual, communal, and institutional renewal. It invites us to service of the ministry of lay people, partnership with them in mission, and openness to creative ways of future cooperation. The Spirit is calling us as "men for and with others" to share with lay men and women what we believe, who we are, and what we have, in creative companionship, for "the help of souls and the greater glory of God."[16]

Another significant document from this congregation was Decree 14, *Jesuits and the Situation of Women in Church and Civil Society*. Calling attention to the many instances of continuing discrimination and prejudice against women in today's world, this Congregation committed the Society in a more formal and explicit way to regard solidarity with women as integral to its mission. It called Jesuits to a conversion of heart that would lead to a careful and sympathetic listening of the experiences of women, and a greater solidarity and collaboration with them in common apostolic ministries.

The most recent Congregation, the Thirty-Fifth General Congregation, was held in Rome in early 2008 and elected Reverend Father Adolfo Nicholás as superior general. While confirming the decrees and directions of the earlier congregations mentioned above, it also drew up decrees on identity, mission, obedience, governance, and collaboration.

4. The Apostolate of Education

While seeking to adapt the Society's apostolic mission to contemporary needs and challenges, these recent General Congregations did not wish to overlook such traditional ministries of the Society as preaching the gospel, fostering sacramental life, giving the exercises, teaching, formation of the clergy, the work of catechetics, the promotion of Christian communities, and evangelizing those who have not heard of Christ. This was particularly true for the educational and intellectual apostolates, which have had a long and distinctive place in Jesuit history.[17]

In 1547, seven years after the Society of Jesus was established, a school was opened by the Jesuits at Messina in Sicily at the request of the city officials. In response to a similar request, a school was established in Palermo two years later. There also arose at this time the increasing need of providing a solid education for younger Jesuits. With the rising number of young men entering the Society in its early years, Saint Ignatius as superior general clearly recognized the need of providing an excellent education for them if the Society was to accomplish its apostolic goal and mission. This led, for example, to the creation of the renowned Jesuit Roman College (later known as the Pontifical Gregorian University, aka "The Greg") in the city of Rome itself in 1551.[18]

The number of schools continued to grow and at the time of Ignatius's death in 1556 there were some thirty-five Jesuit colleges in various parts of Europe. Two hundred years later there were over eight hundred schools run by the Society in Europe, Asia, and Latin America. The nineteenth century witnessed the rapid expansion of Jesuit secondary schools, colleges, and universities in the United States after the establishment of the first Jesuit school at Georgetown in 1789. At the present time in the United States, Jesuit schools number twenty-eight colleges and universities, forty-six secondary schools, and nine inner-city middle schools. In other parts of the world, Jesuits conduct some two hundred secondary schools and one hundred schools of higher education.

The importance of this educational apostolate has been recognized and reaffirmed by recent General Congregations. For example, the Thirty-First General Congregation (1965–66) in its decree, *The Apostolate of Education*, states: "Let Jesuits have a high regard for the apostolate of education as one of the primary ministries of the Society, commended in a special way by the Church in our time."[19]

This was echoed by The Thirty-Fourth General Congregation (1995), which issued the decrees, *The Intellectual Dimension of Jesuit Ministries*; *Jesuit and University Life* and *Secondary, Primary, and Non-formal Education*.

Like all the Society's ministries, the apostolate of education must be nourished by the basic principles of Ignatian spirituality. Among other things, this educational apostolate should help to develop in students a deepening appreciation of the many ways that God can be found in their world, as well as challenging them to use their gifts to benefit others, especially those most in need. Forming "men and women for others" sums up well this lofty goal.

5. Characteristics for Today

The concluding decree of the Thirty-Fourth General Congregation is entitled *Characteristics of Our Way of Proceeding*. The phrase, "Way of Proceeding," was one that Ignatius frequently used in the *Constitutions of the Society of Jesus* and refers to "certain attitudes, values, and patterns of behavior that join together to become what has been called the Jesuit way of proceeding."[20] This Congregation sought to summarize certain characteristics from this way of proceeding that are particularly significant for the new situations and changing ministries of contemporary times. In doing so, this Congregation presents a helpful summary of certain characteristics of Ignatian spirituality that are especially relevant for the carrying out of its mission today. The following is a brief summary of these characteristics.

a. DEEP PERSONAL LOVE FOR JESUS CHRIST

One is to be a companion of Jesus, continually seeking to know him more intimately so as to love him more ardently and follow him more closely. It will be recalled in this context that early in the course of making the spiritual exercises, Ignatius invites the retreatant to turn prayerfully to "Christ our Lord hanging on the Cross before me" and to ask oneself, "What have I done for Christ? What am I doing for Christ? What ought I to do for Christ?" A deep, personal devotion to Jesus must always be the principal characteristic that marks the Jesuit way of proceeding.

b. CONTEMPLATIVE IN ACTION

The God of Ignatius is the God who is at work in all things. Thus, "to discover and join the Lord, laboring to bring everything to its fullness, is central to the Jesuit way of proceeding."[21] This of course cannot be accomplished without an ongoing spirit of prayerful discernment.

c. AN APOSTOLIC BODY IN THE CHURCH

A Jesuit is not a solitary worker in the vineyard. He is a member of an apostolic body of men united as friends in the Lord, however dispersed over the face of the Earth they may be. In this service of the Lord and his church, Jesuits are especially united to the Roman pontiff, available to be sent on the missions he may entrust to them.

d. IN SOLIDARITY WITH THOSE MOST IN NEED

Jesuits today in all their varied ministries must strive to enter into solidarity with the poor, the marginalized, and the voiceless. They, in turn, can help Jesuits live their own call to apostolic poverty and show them "the way to inculturate gospel values in situations where God is forgotten."[22]

e. PARTNERSHIP WITH OTHERS

This cooperation with others is an essential dimension of the contemporary Jesuit way of proceeding, "rooted in the realization that to prepare our complex and divided world for the coming of the Kingdom requires a plurality of gifts, perspectives, and experiences, both international and multicultural."[23]

f. CALLED TO LEARNED MINISTRY

Jesuits today should be aware of the Society's long tradition that sees the need for learning in the service of the faith and the ministry of the Word. For "it is characteristic of a Jesuit that he embodies in creative tension this Ignatian requirement to use all human means, science, art, learning, natural virtue, with a total reliance on divine grace."[24]

g. MEN SENT, ALWAYS AVAILABLE FOR NEW MISSIONS

A spirit of mobility, readiness, and freedom is another basic component of the Jesuit way of proceeding. For a Jesuit is essentially a man on a mission, a mission he receives from the Holy Father and from his own religious superior, but ultimately from Jesus Christ himself.

h. Ever Searching for the *Magis*

This should be the characteristic that permeates all the others. The search for the *magis* is the search for the more, the greater, the more effective. It involves the Jesuit in the search for the ever-greater glory of God, the ever-fuller service of one's neighbor, the more universal good, the more effective apostolic means. The desire for the *magis* marked the life of Saint Ignatius; it should mark the lives of all his followers.

The following prayer of Father Pedro Arrupe (1907–91) sums up this way of proceeding.

> Lord, meditating on "our way of proceeding," I have discovered that the ideal of *our* way of acting is *your* way of acting.
>
> Give me that *sensus Christi* that I may feel with your feeling, with the sentiments of your heart, which basically are love for your Father and love for all men and women.
>
> Teach me how to be compassionate to the suffering, to the poor, the blind, the lame, and the lepers.
>
> Teach us your way so that it becomes our way today, so that we may come closer to the great ideal of St. Ignatius: to be companions of Jesus, collaborators in the work of redemption.[25]

Conclusion

In this chapter and in the previous ones we have been considering the fundamental sources of Ignatian spirituality and their application to the contemporary scene. Their importance cannot be minimized, for they provide an ongoing and indispensable guidance and direction. But the sources of Ignatian spirituality are not confined to these written documents. They are also expressed and given flesh in the lives of individual Jesuits who over the years since the founding of the Society of Jesus have sought to live out these ideals in the witness of their lives. The following chapter provides some brief portraits of the witness and example of various Jesuits from the earliest days of the Society until the present time.

8

PORTRAITS OF JESUITS

1. Two Founding Fathers: Blessed Peter Faber (1506–46) and Saint Francis Xavier (1506–52)

Peter Faber and Francis Xavier had much in common. They were both born in the year 1506 and both came as young men to study at the University of Paris in 1525. Peter Faber was from Savoy (now a part of France) and a simple, farming background, where a good part of his young years was spent shepherding his father's flocks in their Alpine pastures. In sharp contrast, Francis Xavier came from Spain and the family castle of Xavier at Navarre. The two young students met as roommates in the College of Sainte-Barbe at the University of Paris and began a friendship in the Lord that would grow to be a deep and abiding one.

A third roommate and fellow student, Ignatius of Loyola, who had come to Paris as a student from Spain the year before, joined them in 1529. Both were greatly impressed by Ignatius and in the course of time both were drawn to Ignatius's vision and his burning desire to follow Christ totally and faithfully. Peter Faber was the first to come under the spiritual influence of Ignatius, and so he is often referred to as the first disciple or the first recruit of Ignatius. With Ignatius's guidance and direction, Peter Faber made the decision to become a priest, and before ordination he made the full spiritual exercises of thirty days under the direction of Ignatius.

The process of committing himself to Ignatius's spiritual vision required more time for Francis Xavier. But once the decision was made, it was carried out with that fervent sense of love and dedication that marked Xavier's entire life. Tradition has it that Ignatius's words to Xavier were the powerful means God employed to bring Xavier to this commitment: "Francis, what shall it profit a man if he gain the whole world and lose his own soul?"

Peter Faber and Francis Xavier were with Ignatius and four others when the band of seven university students pronounced private vows of poverty and chastity and a resolve to go to the Holy Land after their studies in order to labor for the conversion of infidels. Peter Faber celebrated the vow Mass on the Feast of Our Lady's Assumption, 1534, at the chapel of Saint Denis on the slopes of Montmartre outside of Paris.

Faber and Xavier were among the now ten companions who came together in Venice in 1537. When the voyage to the Holy Land proved to be impossible, they went on to Rome, where they placed themselves at the disposal of the pope for apostolic service. Peter Faber first taught theology and Scripture at Rome's Sapienza College and then spent a year of missionary preaching in Parma. Francis Xavier began preaching in Rome, particularly at the French Church of Saint Louis in that city. Both took part in the deliberations of the founding fathers during Lent of 1539 that led to the formation of the Society of Jesus and the election of Ignatius as superior general.

The establishment of the group as a new religious order in 1540 found Faber and Xavier taking different paths as they were assigned separate apostolic missions. For Faber, the next six years would take him to various towns and cities of Europe, constantly preaching, lecturing, hearing confessions, and giving the spiritual exercises. It would be first to Worms and Regensburg in the Rhineland, then on to Spain, and then back to Germany. Among those to whom he gave the spiritual exercises at Mainz was a young student from Cologne, Peter Canisius, the future Jesuit theologian and apostle to Germany. In 1544 Saint Ignatius sent Faber to Portugal at the request of King John III, and for the next two years he labored in Portugal and Spain. His final assignment came in 1546, when Pope Paul III appointed him one of the papal theologians for the ecumenical council that would take place at Trent. On the way to Trent, he stopped at Rome to see Ignatius, their first meeting in seven years. This would be the last of his many journeys, for a fatal fever struck him down at Rome. In August 1, 1546, this holy and gentle Jesuit returned to Lord he had served so faithfully. His *Memoriale*, the spiritual diary and reflections that he kept during his life, clearly shows that all his journeys and apostolic labors were motivated by a deep love of Christ and a strong desire to serve him generously and steadfastly. Blessed Peter Faber was beatified by Pope Pius IX in 1872, and his memorial is celebrated on August 2.

Peter Faber's apostolic work was extensive, taking him to many towns and cities of Europe, but Francis Xavier's apostolic labors would take him far beyond the confines of Europe. He was the first missionary to the Far East, journeying to foreign lands and places never visited by missionaries. A priest and missionary of amazing zeal and love of God, he was to become the greatest missionary of the church since the time of Saint Paul.

Originally, Francis Xavier was not destined for this missionary role. At the request of Pope Paul III, Ignatius had appointed two of the early Jesuits, Nicholas Bobadilla and Simon Rodriguez, to the Portuguese colony in India that had been recently established. Bobadilla, however, fell sick and Saint Ignatius chose Xavier to take his place. When the ship bound for India finally left Lisbon on April 7, 1541, Xavier set out as the lone Jesuit. At the request of King John III of Portugal, Rodriguez had been reassigned to priestly ministry in Lisbon. Thus, under God's providence, Xavier became the first Jesuit foreign missionary. This missionary activity would come to an end only with his death eleven years later, just off the coast of mainland China.

After a long voyage of thirteen months, Xavier arrived at Goa in India and spent his first five months ministering there and preparing himself for future missionary endeavors. The next two years were spent preaching the gospel and baptizing the Paravas on the Pearl Fishery coast with much success. This was followed by missionary work along India's southeastern shore and a number of East Indian islands, making use of the Portuguese center of Malacca in Malaya as a stopping-off point. It was a meeting at Malacca with a Japanese nobleman that led Xavier to cast his eye on the unknown land of Japan.

Accompanied by two other Jesuits and three Japanese converts, Xavier was finally able to set out for Japan, leaving Malacca on June 24, 1549, and landing at Kagoshima in southern Japan on August 15, the Feast of Mary's Assumption. Two years and three months of difficult missionary work followed, first at Kagoshima and then at Yamaguchi.

Returning to India, Xavier now felt a strong call to concentrate his attention on entering mainland China. By this time there were a number of Jesuits working in India, since Xavier's letters to Europe describing the needs and challenges of missionary work in the East inspired many to follow in his footsteps. At this time, he was also appointed the Jesuit superior of the "Indies and the countries beyond."

Xavier finally began his attempt to penetrate China, leaving India in April 1552 and landing on the desolate island of Sancian in the Bay of Canton in September 1552. He was some six miles from the coast of China, but it proved impossible for him to secure passage to the mainland. A fever struck him down on November 21, and during this final sickness he was cared for by his Christian Chinese interpreter, who fortunately later left an account of Xavier's final days. He writes:

At noon on Thursday he regained his senses, but spoke only to call upon the Blessed Trinity, Father, Son and Holy Ghost, always one of his tenderest devotions. I heard him again repeat the words: *Jesus, Son of David, have mercy on me*, and he exclaimed again and again: *O Virgin Mother of God, remember me!* He continued to have these and similar words on his lips until the night of Friday passed on towards the dawn of Saturday, when I could see that he was dying and put a lighted candle in his hand. Then, with the name of Jesus on his lips he rendered his soul to his Creator and Lord with great repose and quietude.[1]

A lonely and humble death for a great servant of the Lord.

Saint Francis Xavier was beatified by Pope Pius V on October 25, 1619, and canonized by Pope Gregory XV on March 12, 1622, along with his friend and companion in the Lord, Saint Ignatius of Loyola. His feast is celebrated on December 3. In 1925 he was named by Pope Pius XI, together with Saint Thérèse of Lisieux, patron of all missions.

2. Two Theologians and Doctors of the Church: Saint Peter Canisius (1521–97) and Saint Robert Bellarmine (1542–1621)

Saint Peter Canisius, the great apostle to Germany, was born at Nijmegan in the Netherlands in 1521. As a young man, he studied theology at Cologne in Germany for a number of years. He joined the recently founded Society of Jesus in 1543, shortly after making the Ignatian spiritual exercises at Mainz under the direction of Blessed Peter Faber. He completed his theological studies at Cologne and was ordained to the priesthood on June 12, 1546. While at Cologne, he also authored a two-volume work on the fathers of the church that has the distinction of being the first book published by a Jesuit. After serving as a theological consultant for a short time at the Council of Trent, he was assigned by Saint Ignatius to teach at the first Jesuit school to be opened at Messina in Sicily.

After his solemn profession as a Jesuit at Rome in 1549, Peter Canisius returned to Germany to begin the challenging work of restoring and reestablishing the Catholic Church in that country. The church in Germany had been greatly weakened and shaken by the Protestant Reformation and the attacks of the reformers. For the next thirty years Peter Canisius labored steadily and heroically at this enormous task to such an extent that Pope Leo XIII at a later date referred to him as the "Second apostle to Germany after Boniface."

Canisius's apostolate in Germany was carried out by means of preaching, teaching, and writing. He was at Ingolstadt for three years and then moved on to Vienna in 1552. It was at Vienna that he composed the most influential of all his writings, his famous *Catechism* entitled, *A Summary of Christian Doctrine*. It was in the form of questions and answers, with disputed topics with Protestants receiving special attention. The *Catechism* was first published in Latin in 1555 and translated into German a year later. The original *Catechism* was intended for university and college students, but two adaptations of it were soon made for younger students. These catechisms were very successful, for they met a great need. They were used throughout Europe and in mission countries.

Canisius left Vienna in 1555 to open a Jesuit college in Prague. Then in June 1556, shortly before Saint Ignatius's death, he was appointed the first Jesuit provincial superior of the German province. The German province, at the time of his appointment, included

Austria, Hungary, Bavaria, Bohemia, and Swabia. Separate provinces would be formed later as the number of Jesuits grew, but Canisius remained provincial of southern Germany until 1669.

Under Canisius's leadership, the Society grew in Germany and a number of Jesuit colleges were opened. Canisius and the Jesuits he guided as provincials contributed much to the important work of the Counter-Reformation in Germany. After some thirteen years a provincial superior, he went to Innsbruck in Austria, where he continued his work of preaching and writing.

A new and final assignment came to him in 1580 when he was asked to establish a Jesuit college in Fribourg, Switzerland. After the opening of the college in 1582, he remained in Fribourg, again devoting himself to preaching and writing until failing health prevented it. This gentle, humble, and indefatigable laborer in the Lord's vineyard, who did so much for the Catholic revival in Germany, died at Fribourg on December 21, 1597.

Saint Peter Canisius, apostle to Germany, was beatified by Pope Pius IX in 1864 and canonized by Pope Pius XI in 1925. At the time of his canonization, he was also declared a Doctor of the Church (one of only thirty-three). His feast is celebrated on April 27.

Saint Robert Bellarmine, like Peter Canisius, was a towering figure in the Catholic Counter-Reformation. A man of vast learning and simple, genuine holiness, endowed with a warm and engaging personality, he gave himself generously to the service of the church at a critical period. He is widely recognized as the greatest theologian of his age.

After early studies with the Jesuits in his hometown of Montepulciano in Tuscany, Robert Bellarmine entered the Society of Jesus in 1560. As a young Jesuit, he studied philosophy at the Roman College and then taught classics at Florence and Mondovì. Theological studies followed at Padua and Louvain, and he was ordained to the priesthood in 1570.

He began teaching theology at Louvain in Belgium in 1569, the first year at the University of Louvain and then at the newly opened Jesuit theologate for the next six years. Louvain at the time played an important role in the Catholic Church's frontline defense against the Protestant reformers, particularly Martin Luther and John Calvin. In addition to his regular teaching and other work, Bellarmine devoted himself to a careful reading and study of the teaching of the reformers. These studies, and his own profound grasp of Scripture, church history, and patristics, prepared the way for his famous work that would be published later, the *Controversies*.

In 1576, he returned to Rome to assume the chair of "controversial theology" at the Roman College (later called the Gregorian University). His lectures and teaching over the succeeding years led to the publication of his most celebrated work, the *Controversies* (its full title was *Disputations on the Controversies of the Christian Faith Against the Heretics of the Age*), published in three volumes between 1586 and 1593. A work of outstanding scholarship, it was widely read by both Catholics and Protestants and met with great success, passing through more than twenty editions. Before presenting and clarifying Catholic teaching on various disputed issues, Bellarmine carefully summarized and criticized the reformers' teaching in a fair and non-polemical manner, a procedure that was rare in those highly charged times.

A number of other assignments followed this long period of teaching and writing. In 1588 he became the spiritual director for the students at the Roman College and the English College. One of the young Jesuit students at the Roman College at this time was the future saint, Aloysius Gonzaga. A close spiritual bond was formed between these two saints, lasting only a relatively short time, for Aloysius died at the young age of only twenty-three on June 21, 1591. Bellarmine became rector of the Roman College in 1592, and continued his involvement in a number of papal commissions and projects.

In 1594 he left Rome to become provincial superior of the Jesuit province of Naples. His zealous work as provincial came to an end in 1597, when Pope Clement VIII summoned him back to Rome to succeed Cardinal Francesco Toledo as the pope's personal theologian. Two years later, although Bellarmine sought to avoid the honor, Clement made him a cardinal of the church. When he named him a cardinal, the pope noted: "We elect this man because he has not his equal for learning in the church." Bellarmine had to assume some of the external trappings of the position, but in his personal lifestyle, he continued to live very simply.

Somewhat to his own surprise, Cardinal Bellarmine was named archbishop of Capua in 1602. He devoted himself to these new pastoral challenges with the same generosity and commitment that marked his earlier assignments. Three years later, however, a new pope, Paul V, summoned Bellarmine back to Rome to work again for the church at large. He would remain in Rome for the rest of his life, serving on a number of Roman Congregations and advising on the many and varied theological issues that arose.

During his later years, Bellarmine in his writings turned to spiritual themes. These writings flowed from the extended retreat he made each year and included such works as *On the Ascent of the Mind to God* (1614), *The Eternal Happiness of the Saints* (1615), and *The Art of Dying Well* (1620).

Finally, nearing seventy-nine years of age and in declining health, he was able to leave the service of the church and retire to the Jesuit novitiate of Sant'Andrea. Three days later he came down with a fever from which he never recovered. This great and holy servant of God and his church died on September 17, 1621. Saint Robert Bellarmine was canonized by Pope Pius XI in 1923 and a year later he was named a Doctor of the Church. His feast is celebrated on September 17.

3. Three Young Saints: Saint Stanislaus Kostka (1550–68), Saint Aloysius Gonzaga (1568–91), and Saint John Berchmans (1599–1621)

None of the above three Jesuits accomplished what Faber, Xavier, Canisius, or Bellarmine did in their lives. Stanislaus Kostka, Aloysius Gonzaga, and John Berchmans died at the young ages of eighteen, twenty-three, and twenty-two, respectively. Yet God's grace worked so abundantly in their short lives and they cooperated with that grace so generously that they indeed achieved much in a short time.

Born of a noble and distinguished Polish family, Stanislaus Kostka, at the age of fourteen, went with his older brother to study at the recently founded Jesuit school in Vienna. He thrived there as a student, devoting himself to his studies and living an unusually devout life. This proved to be an irritant to his older brother with whom he boarded, and Stanislaus had to endure his bullying behavior. After recovering from a critical illness in which he received the Eucharist in a miraculous way and was consoled by Our Lady who told him that he would enter the Society of Jesus, Stanislaus resolved to apply for the Society.

The Jesuit provincial at Vienna was reluctant to accept him without his family's consent. Knowing that his father would not allow this, Stanislaus followed the advice of another Jesuit and set out for Augsburg, Germany, to request admission from the German provincial, Peter Canisius. After walking the 450 miles to Augsburg and finding that Canisius was at that time in Dillingen, he made another day's journey by foot. The meeting of these two future saints led Canisius to make arrangements for Stanislaus to travel to Rome with two other Jesuits. On foot yet again, Stanislaus made the journey over the Alps to Rome, bearing a letter from Canisius to another future Jesuit saint, Francis Borgia, now superior general of the Society. In his letter of introduction, Peter Canisius writes:

> He is a Polish noble and his name is Stanislaus. He is an excellent, intelligent young man....On his arrival here he was so eager to carry out his long-standing ambition—some years ago he committed himself unreservedly to the Society, though not yet admitted to it....He was very eager to be sent to Rome to be as far away as possible from any harassment by his family. He also wished to advance as much as he could in the path of holiness....We hope for great things from him.[2]

These "great things" that were expected were not to be in God's plan. Stanislaus's novitiate and time as a Jesuit would be less than a year. Taken ill with a fever on August 10, 1569, Stanislaus died a few days later on August 15, the Feast of the Assumption of Mary. His remains now lie in the church in Rome that was attached to the Jesuit novitiate, Sant'Andrea Quirinale. Stanislaus Kostka has the distinction of being the first Jesuit to be beatified (1605). He was canonized by Pope Benedict XIII on December 31, 1726. Patron of Jesuit novices, his feast is celebrated on November 13.

A remarkable family background was part of Aloysius Gonzaga's heritage when he was born on March 9, 1568. His father was the marquis of Castiglione in Lombardy and a prince of the Holy Roman Empire. His mother was a member of the famous and influential Della Rovere family. Both parents were thus related to members of the nobility throughout Europe and to many high churchmen. As the eldest son, Aloysius was the heir to the family title and estates, and his father assumed his son would follow in his footsteps as a military man.

As a young man, Aloysius and his younger brother were exposed to all the glamour, attraction, and temptations of court life at Florence and Mantua. The young Aloysius reacted against this life and intensified a life of prayer, devotion, and penance—an interior life that had deeply attracted him from an early age.

When the Empress Maria of Austria was passing through Italy on a return trip to Madrid from Bohemia in 1581, the Gonzaga family accompanied her on the journey. This led to a two-year stay at Madrid, during which Aloysius and his brother served as pages at the court. During this period, Aloysius made the decision to renounce his heritage and seek admission to the Society of Jesus. It was a decision that led to a protracted struggle with his father, who looked upon this as an abdication of family responsibility. Returning with his family to Castiglione in 1584, Aloysius was sent on a tour of the courts in northern Italy with the hope that this might dissuade him from his strong resolve. Seeing that nothing would deter his son, the father finally gave his permission and the family succession was transferred to the younger brother, Rudolfo.

Aloysius entered the Jesuit novitiate of Sant'Andrea in Rome on November 25, 1585. He was only in his eighteenth year at the time, but a young man mature beyond his years because of his vocational struggles and spirit of commitment. The novitiate was followed by studies in philosophy and theology at the Roman College. His spiritual director at the Roman College was Robert Bellarmine.

In the midst of his studies in preparation for ordination to the priesthood, a plague broke out in Rome. Aloysius volunteered to work with the plague-stricken at the hospital the Jesuits had set up and, while caring for the sick, he himself was infected by the plague. It left him with a lingering sickness and a general weakness of body that led ultimately to his death on June 21, 1591.

Aloysius was buried in the church attached to the Roman College, but later his remains were moved to the newly built church of Saint Ignatius. He was beatified by Pope Paul V in 1605 and canonized together with Saint Stanislaus Kostka by Pope Benedict XIII in 1726. The feast day of this patron of youth is celebrated on June 21.

In contrast to Stanislaus Kostka and Aloysius Gonzaga, who were from aristocratic backgrounds and who were favored with many extraordinary graces and gifts, John Berchmans's road to a life of holiness was far more ordinary. He was born at Diest in Belgium, the eldest son of a shoemaker. He felt drawn to the priesthood from an early age, but finding funds for his continuing education provided a challenge.

After early studies in Diest, he went to Mechlin in 1612 to study at the cathedral school, where he also worked as a servant at the household of the cathedral canon. He transferred to the Jesuit college when it was opened in 1615 and a year later he entered the Jesuit novitiate in Mechlin. From the very beginning of his Jesuit life, he gave himself to all his ordinary tasks and duties with generosity, dedication, and a joyous spirit. This would be the hallmark of the short number of years that would be his as a Jesuit. Holiness would be achieved by doing the ordinary things of his religious life in an extraordinary manner.

The two years of novitiate and the profession of his first vows were followed by studies in philosophy at the Roman College. These three years of study in Rome were marked with that same spirit of faithfulness and dedication that was evident in the novitiate. At the conclusion of his studies in philosophy, John Berchmans was the student chosen to present the customary public defense of the philosophy curriculum, and this was followed by another public disputation at the Greek College as the representative of the Roman College.

These public disputations and the serious study they demanded no doubt weakened his health, for he fell sick shortly afterward. It was to be an illness from which he would not recover, and on August 13, 1621, he passed into eternity. Before his death he asked for his crucifix, rosary, and rule book with the words: "These are the three things most dear to me; with them I willingly die." These words sum up a life that was ordinary in most ways, but extraordinary in the eyes of the God he served so faithfully. John Berchmans was beatified on May 28, 1865, by Blessed Pope Pius IX and canonized by Pope Leo XIII on January 15, 1888.

4. Two Jesuits United in the Lord: Saint Alphonsus Rodríguez (1533–1617) and Saint Peter Claver (1580–1654)

We have already seen how the lives of future Jesuit saints often came together under God's providence. Saint Stanislaus Kostka walked from Vienna to Augsburg and then on to Dillingen in Germany to seek admission into the Society from Saint Peter Canisius. While the young Saint Aloysius Gonzaga was studying theology at the Roman College, he had Saint Robert Bellarmine as his spiritual director. But perhaps the best example of this spiritual bond was that between Saint Alphonsus Rodríguez, the holy and humble Jesuit coadjutor brother, and Saint Peter Claver, the saintly and heroic apostle to the slaves.

Alphonsus Rodríguez was born in 1533 in Segovia, Spain, the son of a prosperous wool merchant. When Peter Faber came to preach a mission in Segovia, he stayed with the Rodríguez family, and while he was there he prepared the ten-year-old Alphonsus for his First Holy Communion. Later, Alphonsus attended the Jesuit college at Alcalá. He had to leave these studies, however, to assume responsibility for the family business after the sudden death of his father. He later married and had three children.

THE IGNATIAN WAY

A number of tragic events subsequently came into the life of Alphonsus. In a relatively short time, his wife and three young children died. In addition to these losses, the wool and cloth business fell upon hard times, and he was forced to give it up. These events led Alphonsus to deepen his life of prayer and penance as he sought God's will in his life. He applied for entrance into the Society of Jesus but was not accepted because of his age, health, and lack of education. Undaunted, he returned to the classroom, and after two years of further education, he again sought admission to the Society. The Jesuits who examined him were still reluctant because of his age and health, but the Jesuit provincial overruled these objections and accepted him as a coadjutor brother.

On January 31, 1571, at the age of thirty-seven, Alphonsus entered the Jesuit novitiate in Spain. Six months later, he was sent to complete his novitiate at the Jesuit College of Montesión in Palma, on the island of Majorca, just off the coast of Spain. He would spend the remaining forty-six years of his life at this same place, serving mainly as the college porter. With a humble, kind, and joyful spirit, he served for years at this post, seeing Christ in all who came to the door. His reputation of holiness and goodness spread, and students and others sought his advice, encouragement, and prayers.

It was a long, uneventful life, filled with prayer and humble service. The spiritual notes that were discovered after his death, however, do reveal the depth of his prayer and the mystical graces with which he was favored. Brother Alphonsus went home to the Lord he had served so faithfully on October 31, 1617. He was beatified by Pope Leo XII in 1825 and canonized by Pope Leo XIII on January 15, 1888. His feast is celebrated on October 31.

Peter Claver came to Majorca in 1605 to begin his philosophical studies at the Jesuit college, shortly after he had finished his novitiate at Terragona in Spain and pronounced his first vows as a Jesuit. It was there at the college of Montesión that the young Jesuit came to meet the now seventy-two-year-old Alphonsus Rodríguez, and a deep spiritual friendship developed between them. Alphonsus recognized Peter's generous heart and high aspirations and suggested that he think about laboring as a missionary in the New World. His suggestion and inspiration found a receptive heart and, after much prayer and reflection, Peter volunteered for missionary work in the New World.

Before completing his studies in theology at Barcelona, Peter set out for Cartegena (now part of Colombia) in the New World on April 15, 1610. The next five years were devoted to completing his theological studies at the Jesuit college at Bogotá and his tertianship at Tunja. In 1615 he returned to Cartegena and was ordained to the priesthood on March 19, 1616, the first Jesuit to be ordained in Cartegena. He immediately began his apostolic work among the slaves who poured into the port. For the rest of his active life he would be in his own words the "slave of the slaves."

The slave trade was well established at this time, and the port of Cartegena played a key role in it. As one of the two major ports of entry, Cartegea was the arrival point for thousands of African slaves each year. The voyage was a terrible ordeal for the slaves, chained to one another throughout the journey and forced to endure inhumane and abusive conditions. Those who did survive the voyage (one-third did not) arrived in a piteous state.

When any slave ship docked at Cartegena, Peter Claver was there to meet it with food, medicine, and other essentials, aided by groups of interpreters and assistants. When he boarded the ship, he first went below to the hot and foulsome holes to minister physically and spiritually to the dying, baptizing them and reaching out to them with kindness and compassion. Then it was to the sick and those whose bodies had suffered the lash that he turned, cleansing and bandaging their wounds and offering them some brandy to help revive them. Once the slaves were moved from the ship to the shore and placed in temporary sheds before their sale, Peter visited them daily, again meeting their physical and spiritual needs. He gave instruction to those who were not baptized, often making use of pictures and other visual aids to bring them to some knowledge of the Christian faith.

For the most part Peter Claver was unable to have further contact with the slaves after they were sold and brought to the distant mines and plantations, but he did visit those plantations that were in the vicinity of Cartegena each year after Easter to be of whatever service he could to the slaves. During the times between the arrival of the slave ships, Peter ministered to those who were in the two hospitals at Cartegena, one for general cases and the other for the lepers. He was also in demand at the prisons, reaching out to those awaiting execution as well as ministering to the regular prisoners.

This heroic work of patient charity would go on year after year for some thirty-five years, until his own health broke down and prevented him from continuing. It was a labor of love that often went unappreciated by many who were quick to criticize his methods, but his life of heroic love was widely recognized and appreciated after his death. This holy man, who saw Christ so clearly in others, especially the outcast and most abandoned, died at Cartegena on September 9, 1554. Peter Claver was beatified by Blessed Pope Pius IX in 1851 and canonized by Pope Leo XIII on January 15, 1888. He was fittingly canonized together with Saint Alphonsus Rodriguez, the saintly Jesuit brother who played such an important role in the life of Peter Claver.

5. Three Martyrs: Saint Edmund Campion (1540–81), Saint Isaac Jogues (1607–46), and Blessed Miguel (Michael) Pro (1891–1927)

The year 1568 was a critical one for Edmund Campion, the brilliant and eloquent Oxford fellow with a promising intellectual and ecclesiastical career before him. He had already distinguished himself as a scholar, orator, and leader at Oxford. When Queen Elizabeth visited the university in 1566, Campion gave a welcoming address in Latin that greatly impressed the queen and the lords, William Cecil and the duke of Leicester. Campion had already taken the Oath of Supremacy, acknowledging the queen as the head of the church rather than the pope, and the year 1568 marked his ordination as a deacon in the Anglican Church. His readings in the church fathers, however, had raised many doubts in his mind about the legitimacy of the Established Church of England and his future as part of it.

After an interim period of teaching and writing in Dublin and a return to England, Campion's wavering came to end in 1572. Realizing that he could no longer stay in England as a Catholic, he made the critical decision to cross the Channel and go as an exile to the English College at Douai in France, recently founded by Father William Allen as a seminary that trained priests for England. At Douai he was officially reconciled to the Roman Catholic Church and then devoted himself to further theological study. After completing a degree in theology, Campion set out for Rome in 1573 with the intention of applying to the Society of Jesus. He was accepted into the Society, but since there was no English province or mission at the time in the Society, he was assigned to the province of Austria.

After completing his novitiate in Brunn and Prague and pronouncing his first vows, Campion was assigned to the Jesuit college in Prague, where he taught rhetoric and philosophy and wrote and directed plays for the students. He was ordained to the priesthood at Prague in 1578. These years of relative calm, however, would soon come to an end. In 1579 the Jesuits were asked by Pope Gregory XIII to open a mission in England, and Edmund Campion was one of the first to be assigned to it. He left Prague in March 1580, and after a short stay in Rome, set out for England with two other Jesuits, Father Robert Persons and Brother Ralph Emerson. On June 24, 1580, disguised as a jewelry merchant, Campion landed at Dover in the England that he had fled some eight years earlier.

Shortly after his arrival, Campion wrote a manifesto to the queen's Privy Council that subsequently became known as *Campion's Brag*. In this stirring document that emphasized that the Jesuit mission to England was for religious, not political, purposes, he ends with the eloquent words: "The expense is reckoned, the enterprise is begun; it is of God, it cannot be withstood. So the faith was planted, so it must be restored."[3]

Campion's ministry to the English Catholics would last little more than a year. As he traveled secretly and in disguise from one household to another, celebrating Mass, preaching, and hearing confessions, he was in constant danger of discovery and arrest. Betrayed finally by a professional priest hunter, Campion was arrested with two other Jesuits and taken to the Tower of London on July 22, 1581.

Campion was given many opportunities to renounce his Catholic faith and return to the queen's service, but he remained firm in his resolve, even after undergoing the tortures of the rack. On November 14, he was convicted of high treason and condemned to be hanged, drawn, and quartered. The words he spoke before the final sentencing on behalf of himself and the other English martyrs still ring out heroically today: "The only thing we have now to say is, that if our religion do make us traitors, we are worthy to be condemned; but otherwise are, and have been, as good subjects as ever the Queen had. In condemning us you condemn all your own ancestors—all the ancient priests, bishops and kings—all that was once the glory of England, the island of saints, and the most devoted child of the See of Peter."[4]

Campion was first dragged by horse through the mud and rain to Tyburn, and then was hanged, drawn, and quartered there on December 1, 1581. This scholar, priest, hero, and martyr was beatified by Pope Leo XIII in 1881 and canonized by Pope Paul VI on October 25, 1970.

Isaac Jogues was one of the North American Martyrs, the eight French Jesuit missionaries who were martyred in North America between the years 1642 and 1649. Six of them were Jesuit priests and two were Jesuit donées (lay missionary assistants). Five were martyred near present-day Midland, Ontario, Canada, and three met their violent deaths in the vicinity of Auriesville, New York. Both places now have shrines in memory of these martyrs and are popular places of pilgrimage. John de Brebeuf (1593–1649) and Isaac Jogues (1607–46) are the best known of the group. Here we focus on Isaac Jogues.

Born at Orléans in France, Isaac Jogues entered the Society of Jesus as a young man of seventeen in 1624. Shortly after his ordination to the priesthood in 1636, the twenty-nine-year-old Jogues set sail for missionary work in New France. By this time there were a number of French Jesuit missionaries in the New World, for a small band of three Jesuits had come to Quebec in Canada as early as 1615. It proved to be one of the most difficult and demanding of all missionary endeavors, for the missionaries had to endure extreme conditions of weather, exposure, and primitive ways of life. They were often objects of suspicion, since natural disasters among the Indian people were often blamed upon them.

Jogues was immediately assigned to the Huron mission and began the challenging missionary work in Huronia, the land where the Hurons settled along the eastern shore of what is now Lake Huron. In June 1642 he traveled with a small group of Hurons to Three Rivers near Quebec to obtain supplies. On the return trip, the group was ambushed and captured by hostile Mohawks. Jogues, along with the other prisoners, suffered savage torture and mutilation before being handed over as a slave to the chief who captured him. After some months of slavery, he was able to escape with the help of the Dutch settlers at Fort Orange (Albany) and arrived back on the coast of Brittany on Christmas morning, 1643. Unable to celebrate Mass in the usual manner because of his mutilated fingers, Father Jogues received a dispensation from Pope Urban VIII, who granted it with the inspiring words, "It would be shameful that a martyr of Christ be not allowed to drink the blood of Christ."

None would have faulted Isaac Jogues if he had remained in France after such labors and sufferings, but in less than four months he set out once more for the mission of New France. Shortly after his return, he took part in the peace negotiations between the French and the Iroquois nations at Three Rivers. Peace terms were reached, but since the approval of the Mohawks was needed, Jogues was sent as an envoy to the Mohawks to obtain their consent. With a successful completion of this mission, Jogues returned to Quebec, hoping that now he would be accepted as a missionary by the Mohawks. The opportunity came in September 1646, when Jogues accompanied some Hurons to the Mohawk center at Ossernenon (Auriesville) to work out some of the details of the peace treaty between the Hurons and Mohawks. Not long after setting out from Quebec, the group learned that the Mohawks were again on the warpath and the Hurons returned to Three Rivers. Hoping for the best, Jogues continued the journey but was soon captured by the Mohawks and taken to their main settlement at Auriesville, where further torture awaited him. Hostility against him ran high since a chest of religious vestments and articles that he had left behind was now blamed for the epidemic that had struck the village. In this atmosphere of heightened dangers Jogues's days were numbered, and on October 18, 1646, he was fatally struck down by a tomahawk at the hands of a Mohawk brave.

Saint Isaac Jogues, together with the other North American Martyrs, was beatified by Pope Pius XI in 1925 and canonized by the same pope on June 21, 1925. The feast of the eight North American Martyrs is celebrated on October 19.

With Miguel Pro, we leave sixteenth-century England and seventeenth-century New France, and come to twentieth-century Mexico. However distant in time, Miguel Pro's life, like the lives of Campion and Jogues, is a tale of faith, courage, and heroism.

Miguel Pro Juárez was born into a large and devout Catholic family in Guadalupe de Zacatecas, Mexico, on January 13, 1891. After finishing his early education, he worked for five years in the office of his father who was a mining engineer. In August 1911, at the age of twenty, he entered the novitiate of the Society of Jesus at El Llano in Michoacán. Completing his novitiate two years later, he pronounced his vows as a Jesuit and remained at El Llano to continue the Jesuit program of studies.

These were times, however, of political and religious turmoil in Mexico, ill-suited for quiet study and prayer. Government leaders were becoming increasingly hostile to religion, and the rebel leader, General Carranza, and the bandit, Pancho Villa, continually harassed and attacked the Catholic Church and the clergy. The Jesuit novices and scholastics at the El Llano were forced to disperse and leave Mexico in August 1914, after soldiers of General Carranza ransacked the novitiate and burned the library. For the next twelve years Miguel Pro lived in exile from Mexico, completing his classical studies at Los Gatos, California, and his study of philosophy at Granada in Spain; teaching for two years in Nicaragua; and studying theology at Sarria in Spain and at Enghien in Belgium. It was at Enghien that he was ordained to the priesthood, at the age of thirty-four, on August 30, 1925. During all of these years he suffered poor health, but this never dampened his zest for life and his upbeat spirit.

After an absence of twelve years, Father Pro returned to Mexico. The country was now an atheistic police state and the Catholic religion was actively persecuted. Shortly after the young priest's return, the government closed all churches and forbade any public worship. This failed to dampen the strong faith of the Mexican people, and Father Pro began a clandestine priestly ministry among them. He established communion stations throughout Mexico City, where he celebrated Mass, heard confessions, and administered the other sacraments. He also preached retreats and reached out in various other ways to those in need. There was no great danger at first, since his long absence from the country had made him an unknown figure to the police. But it grew more and more dangerous as his identity became known. He was forced to assume various disguises to avoid arrest, and the stories of his ingenuity, boldness, and high spirits in avoiding detection became legendary.

This clandestine priestly work lasted only sixteen months, from July 1926 to November 1927. On November 17, Miguel Pro was arrested with his two brothers and falsely charged with plotting to assassinate the presidential candidate, General Alvaro Obregón. Government officials, hoping to intimidate other priests and Catholics, decided to make a public example of Father Pro. On November 23, 1927, he was taken out to the prison yard to face a firing squad, in the presence of a large group of spectators brought together by the government. While awaiting the order for the shots to ring out, Miguel Pro extended his arms in the form of a cross, with his crucifix in one hand and a rosary in the other, and spoke out in a firm voice, "*Viva Christo Rey!* Long Live Christ the King!"

This attempt by the government to frighten other Catholics did not succeed. Thousands came to witness the burial of Miguel

Pro and news of his death spread throughout the world. He soon became one of the best known and revered martyrs of the twentieth century. Father Miguel Pro was beatified by Pope John Paul II on September 25, 1988.

6. Saint Claude la Columbière (1641–82) and Devotion to the Sacred Heart of Jesus

Saint Claude la Columbière was the "faithful servant" whom the Lord, in his providential love, sent to Saint Margaret Mary Alacoque (1647–90) to be her spiritual director and source of support at a critical time in her life. As a Visitation Sister at the convent in Paray-le-Monial, France, she was the recipient of a number of revelations of the Sacred Heart. Saint Margaret Mary and Saint Claude la Columbière were to be the instruments of God for awakening the church to a renewed awareness of God's love symbolized by the Sacred Heart of Jesus.

Claude la Columbière was born in 1641 at Saint-Symphorien d'Ozon, not far from Lyons in France. He entered the Jesuit novitiate at Avignon at the age of seventeen, and after pronouncing his first vows as a Jesuit, he remained at Avignon to study philosophy at the Jesuit College and then to teach grammar and the humanities at the same college. In 1666 he went to the Jesuit College of Clermont in Paris for his theological studies and he was ordained to the priesthood in 1669. After completing these studies in theology, he taught rhetoric for three years in Lyons and served as preacher at the Jesuit church attached to the college for one year. This apostolic work was followed by tertianship, the final year in the formation of a Jesuit and a period of time that focused more on prayer and a renewal of heart. During the tertianship thirty-day retreat, and after much thought and prayer, he was led by God's grace to take the unusual step of making a special vow of complete fidelity to the Rule of the Society of Jesus.

At the conclusion of the tertianship year in 1675, Father Claude la Columbière was appointed superior of the Jesuit house in Paray-le-Monial, and it was here that the lives of two future saints would intersect. Sister Margaret Mary had entered the convent of the Visitation nuns four years before the arrival of Father la Columbière at Paray, and during those years she had experienced a number of visions and private revelations during which Christ requested that the love of God for humanity be more widely recognized. She encountered a certain amount of skepticism and misunderstanding because of these revelations, so she felt a particular need for some solid direction and assurance. Claude la Columbière visited the Visitation convent shortly after his arrival at Paray-le-Monial, and when he was introduced to the community there, Sister Margaret Mary heard an interior voice saying to her: "This is he whom I have sent to you."

In the course of their subsequent spiritual conversations, Claude la Columbière came to recognize the authenticity of Margaret Mary's revelations, and was able to give her the support, assistance, and confirmation that she needed. Together they did much to spread the message of God's love for all men and women. They especially played a key role in responding to the request of the Lord that the Friday following the octave of Corpus Christi be established as a special feast day in honor of the Sacred Heart.

Claude la Columbière's stay at Paray-le-Monial was to be a relatively brief one because in 1676 he was appointed the chaplain and preacher to the duchess of York (the wife of the future James II) at the Queen's Chapel at Saint James Palace in London. Since no English priest could officiate in the country, the chaplain to the duchess had to come from the Continent. Claude la Columbière was eventually caught up in the persecution of priests and he was arrested in November 1678 and imprisoned in a cold dungeon. When his health rapidly declined and he suffered a number of hemorrhages, prison officials decided to send him back to France in January 1679.

Suffering from tuberculosis, he served for a time as spiritual director for the young Jesuits teaching at the college in Lyons. Later, superiors sent him to Paray-le-Monial, hoping that the climate there would benefit his health. Fittingly, it was at Paray that he died peacefully on February 15, 1682. Claude la Columbière, apostle of the Sacred Heart, was beatified by Pope Pius XI in 1929 and canonized by Pope John Paul II on May 31, 1992.

The Society of Jesus and Devotion to the Sacred Heart

Since the time of Saint Claude's death, there has been a close connection between the Society of Jesus and Devotion to the Sacred Heart of Jesus, a relationship that has evolved over the course of the Society's history. On July 2, 1988, Father General Peter-Hans Kolvenbach met at Paray-le-Monial with some three hundred Jesuits from around the world. The occasion marked the three hundredth anniversary of a special apparition of Our Lady to Saint Margaret Mary on the Feast of the Visitation, 1688. On that day, the Society of Jesus received the mission to spread the spirituality of the Sacred Heart of Jesus as a most pleasing gift. In later letters, Saint Margaret Mary confirmed that this mission had been entrusted to her own community, the Visitandines, and to the Society of Jesus.

At this July 2, 1988, meeting at Paray-le-Monial, Father Kolvenbach presented a conference that traced many of the historical highlights of the Society's efforts to fulfill this mission of spreading

Devotion to the Sacred Heart. Only a few of these key aspects will be mentioned here.[5]

A special place of importance, of course, must be given to Saint Claude la Columbière. Christ's love for humanity was a central theme in his preaching and spiritual direction during the few years of apostolic ministry that were left to him after he left Paray-le-Monial to go to England. It was the publication of his retreat notes after his death, moreover, that did much to make known the revelations of Saint Margaret Mary and the Devotion to the Sacred Heart of Jesus. A number of French Jesuits then built upon the foundation of his writings.

The Twenty-Third General Congregation of the Society of Jesus in 1883 solemnly accepted "the most pleasant charge" of propagating the Devotion to the Sacred Heart. Its Decree 46 states "that it should be definitely laid down that the Society of Jesus with the greatest pleasure and deepest gratitude accepts and assumes the most pleasant charge entrusted to her by our Lord Jesus Christ of practicing, fostering and propagating devotion to His most Divine Heart."[6] The decree went on to add that the Feast of the Sacred Heart of Jesus should be considered one of the more solemn feasts in the Society of Jesus, that it should be celebrated with all possible devotion, and that the act of consecration to the Sacred Heart on the part of the Society should be renewed on that day.

Later General Congregations confirmed the Society's close relationship with the Devotion to the Sacred Heart. The Twenty-Sixth General Congregation in 1915 did this explicitly, while also emphasizing that the apostleship of prayer was most suitable for the furthering of this devotion. The Thirty-First General Congregation (1965–66), in its decree *Devotion to the Sacred Heart of Jesus*, confirmed this special mission, stating that "in this way we shall more effectively make the love of Christ, which finds its symbol in the devotion to the Sacred Heart of Jesus, the center of our own spiritual lives, proclaim with greater effect before all men the unfathomable riches of Christ, and foster the primacy of love in the Christian life."[7] It went on to recommend that Jesuit writers seek out ways of presenting this devotion that are better suited for contemporary times, a request that was ably taken up by such eminent theologians as Karl Rahner and Hugo Rahner. There is also the moving, personal message of Father General Pedro Arrupe, in the conclusion of his address and letter, *Rooted and Grounded in Love*. He writes

> From my noviceship on, I have always been convinced that in the so-called devotion to the Sacred Heart there is summed up a symbolic expression of the very core of the Ignatian spirit and an extraordinary power—both for personal perfection and for apostolic fruitfulness. This conviction is still mine today.[8]

During the course of a spiritual pilgrimage to the south of France, Pope John Paul II visited Paray-le-Monial and prayed at the tombs of Saint Margaret Mary and Saint Claude la Columbière on October 5, 1986. At this time he presented to Father Kolvenbach a letter addressed to all Jesuits. He commended the Society for its generosity in accepting and its zeal in carrying out the mission of spreading Devotion to the Sacred Heart. He also wanted to take the opportunity on that solemn occasion "to exhort every member of the Society to promote with even greater zeal this devotion which corresponds more than ever to the expectations of our day." He went on to add that "the desire to know the Lord intimately and to speak heart to heart with him is, thanks to the *Spiritual Exercises*, characteristic of the Ignatian spiritual and apostolic dynamism, totally at the service of the love of the Heart of God."[9]

7. Three Contemporary Jesuits: Pierre Teilhard de Chardin (1881–1955), Walter Ciszek (1904–84), and Pedro Arrupe (1907–91)

April 10, 2005, marked the fiftieth anniversary of the death of the French Jesuit priest and scientist, Pierre Teilhard de Chardin. He followed in the footsteps of such earlier Jesuit priests and scientists as Christopher Clavius (1538–1612), Matteo Ricci (1552–1610), and Athanasius Kirchner (1602–80). His love of God and his love of the world blossomed together into a vocation to be both a Jesuit priest and a geologist. As a priest, scientist, and writer he had much influence upon various areas of Christian theology in the twentieth century. It could be argued, however, that his greatest contribution lies in his rich spirituality of the Christian's role in the world. He was a missionary and an apostle who sought energetically and insistently to unveil the presence of God in the world through the Risen Christ. He sought to proclaim Christ in all his fullness.

Pierre Teilhard de Chardin was born on May 1, 1881, in Sarcenat, France. He attended the Jesuit college of Mongré as a young man and then entered the Jesuit novitiate at Aix-en-Provence in 1899. His early years as a Jesuit took him to many different places. He studied philosophy on the island of Jersey; he taught chemistry and physics as a Jesuit scholastic in Cairo; he studied theology in Hastings, England. After his ordination to the priesthood and the completion of his theological studies in 1912, he began graduate studies in geology at Paris. The outbreak of World War I interrupted these studies, and he served as a stretcher-bearer at the front in the French army for the duration of the war. Some important writings that contain seeds of his later thought flowed from this crucial period of his life. They were later collected and published under the titles of *The Making of a Mind* and *Writings in Time of War*.

The conclusion of the war allowed him to return to Paris to resume his scientific studies. He received his doctorate in 1922 and then taught geology at the Institut Catholique in Paris for the next three years. It was also a time for field trips to China and continued research and writing. In 1925, controversies arose over some of his writings and led his religious superiors to require that he resign his teaching position at Paris and take on a new assignment in China. China would be the principal area of his work for the next twenty years. During this time he became one of the great specialists of East Asian geology and paleontology, and he continued to develop his thought through his extensive writings. He completed his important spiritual work, *The Divine Milieu*, in 1927 and from 1938 to 1940 he wrote his major scientific work, *The Phenomenon of Man*. These two books, like most of his writings, were only published after his death.

In 1951, Teilhard became a scientific associate to the Viking Fund (later the Werner Gren Foundation) for the support and encouragement of anthropological studies. He remained in the position until his death, with the United States as the base of operation for his scholarly work and travel. Death came suddenly to Teilhard on Easter Sunday, March 15, 1955, after suffering a heart attack in New York City. It was fitting in many ways that he died on Easter Sunday because he had always sought to serve and make known the Risen Christ.

Teilhard could reconcile his faith in God and his faith in the world because he was convinced that the Risen Christ is at the center of the world. Since it is Jesus Christ who makes the synthesis between God and the world possible, a personal relationship with the Risen Christ is at the heart of Teilhard's spirituality. For Teilhard, a personal union with Jesus Christ is central to Christian holiness. Yet the direction of this holiness and union with Christ is not away from matter or the world or human activity, but directly into all this toward the Risen Christ. The Christian is called to cooperate with God's plan to unite progressively all things in Christ. Teilhard expresses this in a prayer he composed during World War I when he was in military service:

> Lord Jesus Christ, you truly contain within your gentleness, within your humanity, all the unyielding immensity and grandeur of this world. You are the Center at which all things meet and which stretches out over all things so as to draw them back into itself; I love you for the extensions of your body and soul to the farthest corners of creation through grace, through life, and through matter.[10]

The life story of Father Walter Ciszek is truly amazing. Believed to be long dead, he arrived back in the United States on October 12, 1963, after an absence of almost thirty years. He had lived twenty-three of those years in the Soviet Union, and most of that time he was in prison or at the slave labor camps of Siberia. He later told the tale of his heroic survival in the books, *With God in Russia* (1964) and *He Leadeth Me* (1973).

Not long after entering the Jesuit novitiate at Poughkeepsie, New York, in 1928, Walter Ciszek learned of the letter of Pope Pius XI that called for volunteers to become part of a new Russian center in Rome that was preparing young clerics for missionary work in Russia. When he completed his novitiate and pronounced his first vows in 1930, he volunteered for this Russian mission. After his studies in philosophy were completed at Woodstock College in Maryland, he left for Rome to study theology at the Gregorian University and Russian studies at the Russicum. He learned to say Mass in the Byzantine rite in preparation for his future work and was ordained to the priesthood at Rome in 1937.

It proved to be impossible to send priests to Russia at that time, and so he was first assigned to a Jesuit mission in Albertyn, situated in eastern Poland.

Ciszek was working at this Jesuit mission when war broke out in September 1939 and the Russian army invaded and occupied Albertyn. Disguised as a worker, he accompanied Polish refugees and volunteer workers into Russia, hoping to minister to their spiritual needs. When Germany invaded Russia in June, 1941, he was arrested as a German spy. He was taken to the infamous Lubianka Prison in Moscow and spent some six years in solitary confinement. After enduring long and intense interrogation as a "Vatican spy," he was sentenced to fifteen years of hard labor in the prison camps of Siberia.

Father Ciszek was sent to Siberia in 1946. There he was forced to labor for years and years, either as an outdoor construction worker in the Arctic cold or in the coal and copper mines. Poorly clothed and fed, and living and working in primitive conditions, he somehow managed to survive while also saying Mass secretly and ministering to the spiritual needs of the other prisoners.

His long sentence of enforced hard labor came to end in April 1955, and he was set free. It was a restricted freedom, however, because he had to remain in the villages and towns of Siberia. The following eight years were spent in Norilsk, Krasnoyarsk, and Abakan, where he supported himself as a factory worker or as an auto mechanic. During all these years he privately carried out a priestly ministry, much to the displeasure of the Secret Police who forced him at times to relocate. It was during this time of restricted liberty that he was able to make contact by mail with his sisters in the United States and thus confirm that he was still alive. Then, almost miraculously, he found himself on a plane leaving Moscow for the United States in October 1963! He later learned that he and a young American student were being exchanged for two Soviet spies.

Back in the United States, Father Ciszek was assigned to the John XXIII Center for Eastern Christian Studies at Fordham University. Until his death in 1984 he gave many retreats and counseled and directed many people who came to him. He was frequently asked how he managed to survive the years of imprisonment and suffering and he always answered simply that it was God's Providence. In his inspiring second book, *He Leadeth Me*, he developed this theme in a simple and moving manner.

This holy and faith-filled Jesuit is buried in the Jesuit cemetery at Wernesville, Maryland, a place where he made the last year of his novitiate and pronounced his first vows as a Jesuit. Walter Ciszek has been declared a Servant of God by the Vatican and his cause for beatification is now under consideration.

Pedro Arrupe was the twenty-seventh successor to Saint Ignatius as the superior general of the Society of Jesus.[11] A Basque (like Saint Ignatius himself), he was born in Bilbao, Spain, on November 14, 1907. As a young man, he terminated his medical studies to enter the Society of Jesus at Loyola, Spain, in January 1927. After completing his novitiate and juniorate, he began his philosophical studies. When the new anticlerical Spanish government expelled the Jesuits in 1932, the young Pedro Arrupe first finished his studies in philosophy in Belgium and then studied theology at Valkenburg in the Netherlands, where he was ordained to the priesthood in 1936. A final year of theology was completed at St. Mary's College, Kansas, in the United States and tertianship, the final year of Jesuit formation, was made in Cleveland, Ohio. These times spent in various parts of Europe and the United States did much to prepare him for his future international work as a missionary in Japan and as superior general of Jesuits throughout the world.

During these years of study, Father Arrupe had been doing some special work in the area of medical morality in preparation for future teaching as a professor of moral theology. These plans changed, however, when the request he made earlier was granted and he was assigned in 1938 to the Japanese mission.

His early years in Japan were spent as a parish priest in Yamachuchi. When Japan declared war on the United States in December 1941, he was suspected of espionage and was imprisoned in solitary confinement for over a month. Shortly after his release, he became the master of novices and rector of the novitiate at Nagatsuka, some six miles from Hiroshima. He was at the novitiate when the first atomic bomb fell on Hiroshima on August 6, 1945. Putting his previous medical knowledge to use, he reached out to the victims, and for the next six months the novitiate provided emergency assistance as an improvised medical center.

In 1954 he was named vice provincial of Japan and then provincial superior in 1958 when Japan became a separate Jesuit province. During this period he traveled extensively in Latin America, the United States, and Europe, seeking recruits and funding for the Japanese mission. As provincial he attended the Thirty-First General Congregation that was held in Rome in 1965, and at this time he was elected the twenty-eighth superior general of the Society of Jesus.

Pedro Arrupe's eighteen years as superior general (1965–83) took place during a period of great change and challenge for the church and the Society of Jesus. A man of great faith and love of God, active and energetic, he provided the steady and charismatic leadership that was needed at this critical time in the Society's history. Although the challenges were numerous and ongoing, he faced them with an optimistic and serene spirit that flowed from his deep conviction of God's grace and power working in his life and the divine providential love that guided him. He traveled extensively as superior general, becoming more and more aware of the needs, challenges, and opportunities that marked the Society's apostolic mission in the second half of the twentieth century.

Father Arrupe's letters and conferences to his fellow Jesuits are a rich legacy of his teaching on Ignatian spirituality. A particular desire he had was to return to the original sources of the Ignatian charism and then make application of this charism to the current situation. This was the explicit aim in three of his important addresses: *Our Manner of Proceeding* (1979), *The Trinitarian Inspiration of the Ignatian Charism* (1980), and *Rooted and Grounded in Love* (1981).[12]

While returning to Rome from the Philippines, where he had gone to commemorate the four hundredth anniversary of the Jesuits' arrival in that country, Father Arrupe suffered a cerebral thrombosis at Rome's Fiumicino Airport on August 7, 1981. He was unable to continue in office and, when the Thirty-Third General Congregation convened in 1983, he formally submitted his resignation as superior general. His moving words to the delegates at this time reflect the same acceptance of God's will that marked his years of activity: "More than ever, I now find myself in the hands of God. It is what I have wanted all my life, from my youth. And this is still the one thing I want. But now there is a difference: the initiative is entirely with God. It is indeed a profound spiritual experience to know and feel myself so totally in his hands."[13] Throughout his last years, confined to his infirmary room at the Jesuit generalate in Rome, he patiently lived out this final abandonment to God's will.

Father Pedro Arrupe died on February 5, 1991. He is buried in the Church of the Gesu in Rome, the burial place also of Saint Ignatius of Loyola. His cause for beatification is presently under consideration.

NOTES

Chapter 1

1. Some helpful biographies of Ignatius of Loyola in English are Cándido de Dalmases, SJ, *Ignatius of Loyola Founder of the Jesuits: His Life and Work*, translated by Jerome Aixala, SJ (St. Louis: The Institute of Jesuit Sources, 1985); Paul Dudon, SJ, *St. Ignatius of Loyola*, translated by W. J. Young, SJ (Milwaukee, WI: Bruce Publishing, 1949); André Ravier, *Ignatius of Loyola and the Founding of the Society of Jesus*, translated by Maura Daly, Joan Daly, and Carson Daly (San Francisco: Ignatius Press, 1987); and José Ignacio Tellechea Idígoras, *Ignatius of Loyola, The Pilgrim Saint*, translated, edited, and with a preface by Cornelius Michael Buckley, SJ (Chicago: Loyola University Press, 1994).

2. Among the English translations of this work are *St. Ignatius' Own Story as Told to Luis González da Camara*, translated by William J. Young, SJ (Chicago: Loyola University Press, 1956); *A Pilgrim Journey: The Autobiography of Ignatius of Loyola*, introduction, translation, and commentary by Joseph N. Tylenda, SJ (Wilmington, DE: Michael Glazier, 1985); *A Pilgrim's Testament: The Memoirs of St. Ignatius of Loyola*, translated by Parmananda R. Divarkar (Rome: Gregorian Press, 1983).

3. Much of the material in this chapter appeared earlier in my treatment of St. Ignatius in *Christian Spirituality, An Introduction to the Heritage* (New York: Alba House, 1999).

Chapter 2

1. See James Brodrick, SJ, *The Origins of the Jesuits* (Chicago: Loyola University Press, 1986), pp. 94–95.

2. See André Ravier, SJ, *Ignatius of Loyola and the Founding of the Society of Jesus* (San Francisco: Ignatius Press, 1987), p. 119.

3. Important historical documents that are in this tradition are the reports sent back to France by the Jesuit missionaries in Northern America in the seventeenth century. See *Jesuit Relations and Allied Documents*, edited by Reuben Gold Thwaites, 73 vols. (Cleveland, 1896–1903).

4. See Ignatius of Loyola, *Spiritual Exercises and Selected Writings*, edited by George Ganss, SJ (Mahwah, NJ/New York: Paulist Press, 1991), p. 50.

5. Ibid., p. 325.

6. See Joseph deGuibert, SJ, *The Jesuits, Their Spiritual Doctrine and Practice*, translated by William Young, SJ (Chicago: Institute of Jesuit Sources, 1964), pp. 84–85.

7. See Harvey D. Egan, SJ, *Ignatius Loyola the Mystic* (Wilmington, DE: Michael Glazier, 1987), p. 19.

8. See *St. Ignatius' Own Story*, translated by William J. Young, SJ (Chicago: Loyola University Press, 1956), #30.

9. Ibid., #95.

10. Ibid., #96.

11. For an English translation, see "The Spiritual Journal of St. Ignatius of Loyola, Feb. 2, 1544 to Feb. 27, 1545," translated by William J. Young, SJ, *Woodstock Letters* 87 (1958): 195–267.

12. DeGuibert, *The Jesuits*, p. 44.
13. Ibid., p. 181.

Chapter 3

1. There are a number of English translations of the *Spiritual Exercises*. References in this chapter will be to *The Spiritual Exercises of Saint Ignatius*, translation and commentary by George E. Ganss, SJ (St. Louis: The Institute of Jesuit Sources, 1992). Father Ganss's extensive notes in this edition are very helpful. Other English translations are *The Spiritual Exercises of St. Ignatius*, a new translation based on studies on the language of the *Autograph*, by Louis J. Puhl, SJ (Chicago: Loyola University Press, 1968); and *Draw Me Into Your Friendship, A Literal Translation and A Contemporary Reading of the Spiritual Exercises*, by David Fleming, SJ (St. Louis: The Institute of Jesuit Sources, 1996).

2. For the importance of the exercises in the ministries of the early Jesuits, see John O'Malley, SJ, *The First Jesuits* (Cambridge, MA: Harvard University Press, 1998), p. 127ff.

3. See Charles J. Healey, SJ, *Christian Spirituality, An Introduction to the Heritage* (New York: Alba House, 1999), p. 254. A parallel can be drawn with the Rule of St. Benedict. Before Benedict composed his famous Rule for monks, there were a number of other monastic Rules in existence in Europe. Benedict learned from these earlier Rules and built upon them in composing the spiritual classic that gradually surpassed and supplanted the earlier Rules that were part of the historical developments in Western monasticism.

4. See, for example, the triple colloquy suggested at the end of the meditation on personal sin (#63) and the meditation on the *Two Standards* (#147).

5. *Spiritual Exercises* #1. All references to the *Spiritual Exercises* will be done by giving the standard paragraph number using the

edition, *The Spiritual Exercises of Saint Ignatius*, translation and commentary by George E. Ganss, SJ (St. Louis: The Institute of Jesuit Sources, 1992).

6. These suggestions are given in annotations 6–10 and 13–14. Ignatius gives rules for the discernment of spirits that are applicable to the First Week and rules that are applicable to the Second Week. More is said about these rules in the chapter on discernment.

7. As we will see later when treating Ignatian methods of prayer, the general examen (or examen of consciousness as it is often called today) has received renewed attention.

8. David L. Fleming, SJ, "The Ignatian Spiritual Exercises: Understanding a Dynamic," in *Notes on the Spiritual Exercises of St. Ignatius of Loyola* (St. Louis, 1981), p. 11.

9. See Ganss, *The Spiritual Exercises*, p. 175.

10. Ibid.

Chapter 4

1. I have found very helpful for this chapter the book by Alexandre Brou, SJ, *Ignatian Methods of Prayer*, translated by William J. Young, SJ (Milwaukee, WI: Bruce Publishing, 1949).

2. For this method of prayer, in addition to Brou, *Methods*, pp. 109–22, see also I. Classen, SJ, "The Exercise with the Three Powers of the Soul," in *Ignatius, His Personality and Spiritual Heritage*, edited by Friedrich Wulf, SJ (St. Louis: The Institute of Jesuit Sources, 1977), pp. 237–71.

3. Brou, *Methods*, p. 116. John Henry Newman's distinction in his *Grammar of Ascent* between notional and real knowledge and his emphasis on the process of realization should be noted in this connection. Realization for Newman involves opening one's mind to a truth, in the sense of bringing the truth into one's conscious-

ness, dwelling upon it, contemplating it vividly, and bringing it home to oneself. It involves opening one's heart to a truth and responding with one's entire being.

4. Ibid., p. 123.

5. See Alexandre Brou, *The Ignatian Way to God*, translated by William J. Young, SJ (Milwaukee, WI: Bruce Publishing, 1952), p. 21. Reference is to #2 of the *Spiritual Exercises*.

6. See *Spiritual Exercises*, ##101–19 for a treatment of Ignatian contemplation. See also Brou, *Methods*, pp. 130–45.

7. For this method of prayer. see Brou, *Methods*, pp. 146–67. See also H. Coathalem, SJ, *Ignatian Insights* (Taichung, Taiwan, 1971), pp. 153–58.

8. Brou in the pages cited in the previous note treats these interpretations more at length. Polanco, a close collaborator of Saint Ignatius, makes a distinction between the bodily or imaginative senses and the spiritual senses, developed by Saint Bonaventure. The first are more suitable for those less experienced in prayer and the latter for those more advanced. Thus he speaks of two applications of the senses, that of beginners and that of souls more advanced. See Brou, *Methods*, pp. 197–98.

9. See the eighteenth introductory annotation in the *Spiritual Exercises*, #18.

10. For an excellent treatment of the Jesus Prayer, see I. Hausherr, SJ, *The Name of Jesus* (Kalamazoo: Cistercian Studies, 1978), pp. 241–347.

11. See the influential and insightful article "Consciousness Examen" by George A. Aschenbrenner, SJ, in *Review for Religious* 31 (1972): 13–21. See also the article by David Keith Townsend, SJ, "The Examen Re-Examined," *Centrum Ignatianum Spiritualitatis* 18, 2 (1987): 11–64.

12. Quoted in Brou, *Methods*, p. 32.

Chapter 5

1. For these historical developments, see Malatesta et al., *Discernment of Spirits* (a translation of the article "Discernment des Esprits" in the *Dictionnaire de Spiritualité*) translated by Sister Innocentia Richards (Collegeville, MN: The Liturgical Press, 1970).

2. John Futrell, SJ, "Ignatian Discernment," *Studies in the Spirituality of Jesuits* 2, 2 (1970): 47.

3. References to this work in this chapter will be to *St. Ignatius' Own Story*, as told to Luis González de Camara, translated by William J. Young, SJ (Chicago: Loyola University Press, 1956).

4. Ibid., no. 8.

5. Ibid., no. 27.

6. For an insightful treatment of the significance of this experience as a unifying principle of discernment, see Leonardo Silos, SJ, "Cardoner in the Life of St. Ignatius of Loyola," *Archivum Historicum Societatis Jesu* 3 (1964): 3–43.

7. The document narrating the process of their discussions is known as "The Deliberation of the First Fathers." English translations of this document can be found in Dominic Maruca, SJ, "The Deliberations of Our First Fathers," *Woodstock Letters* 95 (1966): 325–33, and John C. Futrell, SJ, *Making An Apostolic Community of Love* (St. Louis: The Institute of Jesuit Sources, 1970), pp. 188–94.

8. For a careful study, see the two books by Jules Toner, SJ, *A Commentary on Saint Ignatius' Rules for the Discernment of Spirits: A Guide to the Principles and Practice* (St. Louis: The Institute of Jesuit Sources, 1982); and *Discerning God's Will: Ignatius of Loyola's Teaching on Christian Decision-Making* (St. Louis: The Institute of Jesuit Sources, 1991).

9. All references will be from *The Spiritual Exercises of Saint Ignatius, A Translation and Commentary* by George E. Ganss, SJ (St. Louis: The Institute of Jesuit Sources, 1992).

10. See the observations by Ganss, *The Spiritual Exercises*, p. 194.

11. See *St. Ignatius' Own Story*, ##45–47.

12. See *Letters of St. Ignatius of Loyola*, selected and translated by William J. Young, SJ (Chicago: Loyola University Press, 1959), p. 19.

13. For a helpful treatment of these ideas, see Richard J. Hauser, SJ, *Moving in the Spirit, Becoming a Contemplative in Action* (Mahwah, NJ/New York: Paulist Press, 1986). See also William A. Barry, SJ, *Paying Attention to God* (Notre Dame, IN: Ave Maria Press, 1990); and John J. English, SJ, *Spiritual Freedom: From an Experience of the Ignatian Exercises to the Art of Spiritual Direction*, Second Edition (Guelph, ON: Loyola House, 1982).

14. See the author's "Prayer, the Context of Discernment," *Review for Religious* 33 (1974): 265–70.

Chapter 6

1. See, for example, Joseph deGuibert, SJ, *The Jesuits, Their Spiritual Doctrine and Practice. A Historical Study*, translated by W. J. Young, SJ (Chicago: The Institute of Jesuit Sources, 1964), p. 139.

2. See the introduction of George Ganss, SJ, in *The Constitutions of the Society of Jesus*, translated with an introduction and a commentary by George E. Ganss, SJ (St. Louis: The Institute of Jesuit Sources, 1970), p. 8. For this chapter I am greatly indebted to Father Ganss's careful and scholarly work.

3. Ibid., p. 25.

4. For these points, see ibid., pp. 50–51.

5. *The Constitutions of the Society of Jesus and Their Complementary Norms*, a complete English translation of the official Latin texts, John W. Padberg, SJ, General Editor (St. Louis: The Institute of Jesuit Sources, 1996), #137 (p. 60). All future references

to the *Constitutions* will be taken from this latest and authoritative English translation according to the standard numbering.

6. This is the case in the English edition cited above. See ibid., ##1–9.

7. See also the clarification of this in the *Complementary Norms*, #225.

8. On this passage, see the note by Ganss, *Constitutions*, p. 309.

9. See ##723–33 in the *Constitutions* for the full text. The above is only a brief summary.

10. Very Reverend Peter-Hans Kolvenback, SJ, superior general, in his preface to *The Constitutions of the Society of Jesus and Their Complementary Norms* (St. Louis: The Institute of Jesuit Sources, 1996), p. xii. This preface is helpful for the above points as is the foreword of the general editor, John W. Padberg, SJ.

11. Ibid.

Chapter 7

1. See, for example, Giles Cusson, SJ, *The Spiritual Exercises Made in Everyday Life: A Method and a Biblical Interpretation* (St. Louis, 1989); Joseph A. Tetlow, SJ, *Choosing Christ in the World: Directing the Exercises according to Annotations Eighteen and Nineteen: A Handbook* (St. Louis, 1989); and James W. Skehan, SJ, *Place Me With Your Son, Ignatian Spirituality in Everyday Life* (Washington, DC: Georgetown University Press, 1991). Note should also be made of the growing number of web sites on the internet that provide much helpful material for various forms of retreats in everyday life. Among them are Online Ministries at Creighton University, www.creighton.edu/Collaborative Ministry/online.html and the Irish Jesuits' www.sacredspace.ie.

2. See, for example, William A. M. Peters, SJ, *The Spiritual Exercises of St. Ignatius, Exposition and Interpretation* (Jersey City:

Program to Adapt the Spiritual Exercises, 1967). For a good treatment of the essential aim of the Spiritual Exercises, see Joseph deGuibert, SJ, *The Jesuits, Their Spiritual Doctrine and Practice. A Historical Study*, translated by William Young, SJ (Chicago: Institute of Jesuit Sources, 1964), pp. 122–32.

3. Thirty-First General Congregation, Decree 4, #44. See *Documents of the 31st and 32nd General Congregations of the Society of Jesus* (St. Louis: The Institute of Jesuit Sources, 1977). Any further references to these documents will be from this source with the General Congregation (GC no.), pertinent decree, and continuous number cited.

4. Ibid., Decree 14, #213.

5. Ibid., GC 32, Decree 4, #87.

6. Ibid., GC 32, Decree 4, #107.

7. See the treatment of the general examen in chapter 4.

8. GC 32, Decree 2, #24.

9. GC 31, Decree 1, #1.

10. Ibid., Decree 21, #365.

11. GC 32, Decree 4, #48.

12. Ibid., Decree 2, #11 and 12.

13. GC 33, Decree 1, #11. See *Documents of the 33rd General Congregation of the Society of Jesus* (St. Louis: The Institute of Jesuit Sources, 1984). Any further reference to this congregation will be from this source with the General Congregation (GC no.), pertinent decree, and continuous number cited.

14. Ibid., Decree 1, #54.

15. GC 34, Decree 2, #48. See *Documents of the 34th General Congregation of the Society of Jesus* (St. Louis: The Institute of Jesuit Sources, 1995). Future references to this congregation will be to this source.

16. Ibid., Decree 13, #360.

17. See GC 33, Decree 1, ##46–47.

18. For this, see Philip Caraman, SJ, *University of the Nations, The Story of the Gregorian University of Rome from 1551 to Vatican II* (Mahwah, NJ/New York: Paulist Press, 1981).

19. GC 31, Decree 28, #505.

20. GC 34, Decree 26, #535, 542.

21. Ibid., #542.

22. Ibid., #548.

23. Ibid., #549.

24. Ibid., #553.

25. Ibid., #563. This prayer was taken from an address of Father Arrupe's entitled "Our Way of Proceeding."

Chapter 8

1. Cited from the *Monumenta Xaveriana*, by James Brodrick, SJ, *Saint Francis Xavier* (New York: The Wickloo Press, 1952), p. 562.

2. See Joseph N. Tylenda, SJ, *Jesuit Saints and Martyrs* (Chicago: Loyola Press, 1998), p. 384.

3. See Evelyn Waugh's *Edmund Campion, Jesuit and Martyr* (New York: Doubleday Image Book, 1946), pp. 117–18.

4. Ibid., p. 182.

5. The text of Father Kolvenbach's homily and conference can be found in the Special Edition of Prayer and Service published by the General Office of the Apostleship of Prayer in Rome. The booklet is entitled *A Most Pleasant Mission*. In addition to the homily and conference, it contains the full text of the references made by Father Kolvenbach in his conference. Further notes will be to this source.

6. Ibid., p. 44.

7. Ibid., p. 47.

8. Ibid., p. 53. See also Pedro Arrupe, SJ, *In Him Alone is Our Hope, Texts on the Heart of Christ*, foreword by Karl Rahner, SJ (St. Louis: The Institute of Jesuit Sources, 1984).

9. Ibid., pp. 58–59.

10. See Teilhard's "Cosmic Life," in *Writings in Time of War* (New York: Harper Touchback, 1965), pp. 69–70.

11. For some details of Father Arrupe's life, see Pedro Arrupe, SJ, *One Jesuit's Spiritual Journey*, autobiographical conversations with Jean-Claude Dietsch, SJ, translated by Ruth Bradley (St. Louis: The Institute of Jesuit Sources, 1986).

12. For some of Father Arrupe's writings, see *Pedro Arrupe, Essential Writings*, selected with an introduction by Kevin Burke, SJ (Maryknoll, NY: Orbis Books, 2004).

13. See *Documents of the 33rd General Congregation of the Society of Jesus* (St. Louis: The Institute of Jesuit Sources, 1984), p. 93.

SELECTED BIBLIOGRAPHY

1. Writings of Saint Ignatius Loyola

The Constitutions of the Society of Jesus. Translated, with an introduction and a commentary, by George E. Ganss, SJ. St. Louis: The Institute of Jesuit Sources, 1970.

The Constitutions of the Society of Jesus And Their Complementary Norms. A Complete English Translation of the Official Latin Texts. John W. Padberg, SJ, General Editor. St. Louis: The Institute of Jesuit Sources, 1996.

Counsels for Jesuits: Selected Letters and Instructions of Saint Ignatius of Loyola. Edited by Joseph N. Tylenda, SJ. Chicago: Loyola University Press, 1985.

Draw Me Into Your Friendship. A Literal Translation and A Contemporary Reading of The Spiritual Exercises by David Fleming, SJ. St. Louis: The Institute of Jesuit Sources, 1996.

Ignatius of Loyola, The Spiritual Exercises and Selected Works. Edited by George E. Ganss, SJ. Mahwah, NJ: Paulist Press, 1991.

Letters of St. Ignatius of Loyola. Selected and translated by William J. Young, SJ. Chicago: Loyola University Press, 1958.

A Pilgrim's Journey; The Autobiography of Ignatius of Loyola. Introduction, translation, and commentary by Joseph N. Tylenda, SJ. Wilmington, DE: Michael Glazier, 1985.

Saint Ignatius Loyola, Letters to Women, by Hugo Rahner. Translated by Kathleen Pond and S. A. H. Weetman. New York: Herder and Herder, 1960.

St. Ignatius of Loyola: Personal Writings. Translation with introductions and notes by Joseph A. Munitiz, SJ, and Philip Endean, SJ. London: Penguin Books, 1996.

St. Ignatius' Own Story as Told to Luis González da Camara. Translated by William J. Young, SJ. Chicago: Loyola University Press, 1968.

The Spiritual Exercises of St. Ignatius. A new translation based on studies on the language of the *Autograph*, by Louis J. Puhl, SJ. Chicago: Loyola University Press, 1968.

The Spiritual Exercises of Saint Ignatius. Translation and commentary by George E. Ganss, SJ. St. Louis: The Institute of Jesuit Sources, 1992.

The Spiritual Journal of St. Ignatius of Loyola, February 2, 1544 to February 27, 1545. Translated by William J. Young, SJ. *Woodstock Letters* 87 (1958): 195–267.

2. General Works

Arrupe, Pedro, SJ. *In Him Alone Is Our Hope*. Texts on the Heart of Christ (1965–83). Foreword by Karl Rahner, SJ. St. Louis: The Institute of Jesuit Sources, 1984.

———. *One Jesuit's Spiritual Journey*. Autobiographical conversations with Jean-Claude Dietsch, SJ, translated by Ruth Bradley. St. Louis: The Institute of Jesuit Sources, 1986.

———. *Essential Writings*. Selected with an introduction by Kevin Burke, SJ. Maryknoll, NY: Orbis Books, 2004.

Aschenbrenner, George A., SJ. "Consciousness Examen." *Review for Religious* 31 (1972): 13–21.

————. *Stretched for Greater Glory: What to Expect from the Spiritual Exercises*. Chicago: Loyola Press, 2004.

Barry, William A., SJ. *Paying Attention to God*. Notre Dame, IN: Ave Maria Press, 1990.

————. *Finding God in All Things, A Companion to the Spiritual Exercises of St. Ignatius*. Notre Dame, IN: Ave Maria Press, 1991.

————, and Robert G. Doherty, SJ. *Contemplatives in Action, The Jesuit Way*. Mahwah, NJ: Paulist Press, 2002.

Brodrick, James, SJ. *St. Ignatius of Loyola: The Pilgrim Years*. New York: Farrar, Straus & Cudahy, 1956. (Father Brodrick also has excellent biographies of Saint Francis Xavier, Saint Peter Canisius, and Saint Robert Bellarmine.)

————. *The Origin of the Jesuits*. Chicago: Loyola Press, 2000.

Brou, Alexandre, SJ. *Ignatian Methods of Prayer*. Translated by William J. Young, SJ. Milwaukee, MI: Bruce Publishing, 1949.

————. *The Ignatian Way to God*. Translated by William J. Young, SJ. Milwaukee, WI: Bruce Publishing, 1952.

Byron, William J., SJ. *Jesuit Saturdays: Sharing the Ignatian Spirit with Lay Colleagues and Friends*. Chicago: Loyola Press, 2000.

Caraman, Philip, SJ. *Ignatius of Loyola, A Biography of the Founder of the Jesuits*. San Francisco: Harper and Row, 1990.

Ciszek, Walter, SJ (with Daniel Flaherty, SJ). *He Leadeth Me*. Garden City, NY: Doubleday & Company, 1973.

Clancy, Thomas H., SJ. *An Introduction to Jesuit Life: The Constitutions and History Through 435 Years*. St. Louis: The Institute of Jesuit Sources, 1976.

————. *The Conversational Word of God: A Commentary on the Doctrine of St. Ignatius Concerning Spiritual Conversation*. St. Louis: The Institute of Jesuit Sources, 1978.

Coathalem, Hervé, SJ. *Ignatian Insights*. Translated by Charles J. McCarthy, SJ. Taiwan: Kuangchi, 1961.

Conroy, Maureen. *The Discerning Heart: Discovering a Personal God*. Chicago: Loyola University Press, 1993.

Cowan, Marian, and John C. Futrell. *Companions in Grace: A Handbook for Directors of the Spiritual Exercises of St. Ignatius of Loyola*. Kansas City, MO: Sheed and Ward, 1993.

Cusson, Giles, SJ. *Biblical Theology and the Spiritual Exercises*. St. Louis: The Institute of Jesuit Sources, 1988.

————. *The Spiritual Exercises Made in Everyday Life: A Method and a Biblical Interpretation*. Translated by Mary Angela Roduit and George E. Ganss, SJ. St. Louis: The Institute of Jesuit Sources, 1989.

Dalmases, Cándido de, SJ. *Ignatius of Loyola. Founder of the Jesuits*. Translated by Jerome Aixalá, SJ. St. Louis: The Institute of Jesuit Sources, 1985.

Dudon, Paul, SJ. *St. Ignatius of Loyola*. Translated by Walter J. Young, SJ. Milwaukee, WI: Bruce Publishing, 1949.

Egan, Harvey, SJ. *The Spiritual Exercises and the Ignatian Mystical Horizon*. St. Louis: The Institute of Jesuit Sources, 1976.

————. *Ignatius Loyola the Mystic*. Wilmington, DE: Michael Glazier, 1987.

English, John J., SJ. *Spiritual Freedom: From an Experience of the Ignatian Exercises to the Art of Spiritual Direction*. Second Edition. Guelph, ON: Loyola House, 1982.

Fleming, David L., SJ (ed.). *Notes on the Spiritual Exercises of St. Ignatius of Loyola*. St. Louis: Review for Religious, 1981.

————. *Like the Lighting: The Dynamics of the Ignatian Exercises*. St. Louis: The Institute of Jesuit Sources, 2004.

Gallagher, Timothy M., OMV. *The Discernment of Spirits*. New York: Crossroad, 2005.

————. *Spiritual Consolation: An Ignatian Guide for the Greater Discernment of Spirits*. New York: Crossroad, 2007.

Green, Thomas H., SJ. *Weeds Among the Wheat: Discernment, Where Prayer and Action Meet*. Notre Dame, IN: Ave Maria Press, 1983.

SELECTED BIBLIOGRAPHY

Guibert, Joseph de, SJ. *The Jesuits, Their Spiritual Doctrine and Practice. A Historical Study.* Translated by William J. Young, SJ. St. Louis: The Institute of Jesuit Sources, 1972.

Hauser, Richard, SJ. *Moving in the Spirit, Becoming a Contemplative in Action.* New York: Paulist Press, 1986.

Healey, Charles J., SJ. *Christian Spirituality, An Introduction to the Heritage.* New York: Alba House, 1999.

Hebblethwaite, Margaret. *The Way of St. Ignatius: Finding God in All Things.* Second Edition. London: Fount, 1999.

Idígoras, José Ignacio Tellechea. *Ignatius of Loyola, The Pilgrim Saint.* Translated, edited, and with a preface by Cornelius Buckley, SJ. Chicago: Loyola University Press, 1994.

Ivens, Michael, SJ. *Understanding the Spiritual Exercises: A Handbook for Retreat Directors.* Text and commentary. Leominster, UK: Gracewing, 1998.

Kolvenbach, Peter-Hans, SJ. *The Road from La Storta.* St. Louis: The Institute of Jesuit Sources, 2000.

Lonsdale, David, *Dance to the Music of the Spirit: The Art of Discernment.* London: Darton, Longman and Todd, 1992.

————. *Eyes to See, Ears to Hear, An Introduction to Ignatian Spirituality.* Maryknoll, NY: Orbis Books, 2000.

Martin, James, SJ. *In Good Company: The Fast Track from the Corporate World to Poverty, Chastity and Obedience.* Franklin, WI: Sheed and Ward, 2000.

————. *My Life with the Saints.* Chicago: Loyola Press, 2007.

Meisner, William W., SJ. *Ignatius of Loyola: The Psychology of a Saint.* New Haven: Yale University Press, 1992.

Mueller, Joan. *Faithful Listening, Discernment in Everyday Life.* Kansas City, MO: Sheed and Ward, 1996.

Muldoon, Timothy. *The Ignatian Workout, Daily Spiritual; Exercises for a Healthy Faith.* Chicago: Loyola Press, 2004.

O'Malley, John, SJ. *The First Jesuits.* Cambridge, MA, and London: Harvard University Press, 1993.

O'Malley, William J., SJ. *The Fifth Week*. Second Edition. Chicago: Loyola University Press, 1996.

Peters, William A. M., SJ. *The Spiritual Exercises of St. Ignatius: Exposition and Interpretation*. Rome: Centrum Ignatianum Spiritualitatis, 1978.

Rahner, Hugo, SJ. *Ignatius the Theologian*. Translated by Michael Barry. New York: Herder and Herder, 1968.

Sheldrake, Philip (ed.). *The Way of Ignatius Loyola: Contemporary Approaches to the Spiritual Exercises*. London: SPCK, 1991.

Silf, Margaret. *Inner Compass: An Invitation to Ignatian Spirituality*. Chicago: Loyola Press, 1999.

Skehan, James W., SJ. *Place Me With Your Son, Ignatian Spirituality in Everyday Life*. Third Edition. Washington, DC: Georgetown University Press, 1991.

Tetlow, Joseph, SJ. *Choosing Christ in the World, Directing the Spiritual Exercises of St. Ignatius Loyola According to Annotations Eighteen and Nineteen*. St. Louis: The Institute of Jesuit Sources, 1989.

Toner, Jules L., SJ. *A Commentary on St. Ignatius' Rules for the Discernment of Spirits*. St. Louis: The Institute of Jesuit Sources. 1981.

———. *Discerning God's Will: Ignatius of Loyola's Teaching on Christian Decision Making*. St. Louis: The Institute of Jesuit Sources, 1991.

Veltrie, John, SJ. *Orientations*, vol. 1, *A Collection of Helps for Prayer*. Guelph, ON: Loyola House, 1993.

———. *Orientations*, vol. 2, *For Those who Accompany Others on Their Inward Journey*. Guelph, ON: Loyola House, 1998.

Waugh, Evelyn. *Edmund Campion*. Garden City, NY: Image Books, 1946.

Wulf, Friedrich, SJ (ed.). *Ignatius of Loyola, His Personality and Spiritual Heritage*. St. Louis: The Institute of Jesuit Sources, 1977.

SELECTED BIBLIOGRAPHY

Helpful sources for ongoing articles and essays on Ignatian spirituality are Studies in the Spirituality of Jesuits (publications of the Seminar on Jesuit Spirituality, St. Louis) and *The Way* (and *The Way* Supplements), an international journal of Contemporary Christian Spirituality published quarterly by the British Jesuits.

Helpful also are the websites of Creighton University's "Online Ministries" www.creighton.edu/CollaborativeMinistry/online.html and the Irish Jesuits' www.sacredspace.ie.